Introducing Azure Bot Service

Building Bots for Business

Charles Waghmare

Apress®

Introducing Azure Bot Service: Building Bots for Business

Charles Waghmare
Mumbai, India

ISBN-13 (pbk): 978-1-4842-4887-4   ISBN-13 (electronic): 978-1-4842-4888-1
https://doi.org/10.1007/978-1-4842-4888-1

Copyright © 2019 by Charles Waghmare

Managing Director, Apress Media LLC: Welmoed Spahr
Acquisitions Editor: Smriti Srivastava
Development Editor: Matthew Moodie
Coordinating Editor: Shrikant Vishwakarma

Cover designed by eStudioCalamar

Cover image designed by Freepik (www.freepik.com)

Distributed to the book trade worldwide by Springer Science+Business Media New York, 233 Spring Street, 6th Floor, New York, NY 10013. Phone 1-800-SPRINGER, fax (201) 348-4505, e-mail orders-ny@springer-sbm.com, or visit www.springeronline.com. Apress Media, LLC is a California LLC and the sole member (owner) is Springer Science + Business Media Finance Inc (SSBM Finance Inc). SSBM Finance Inc is a **Delaware** corporation.

For information on translations, please e-mail rights@apress.com, or visit http://www.apress.com/rights-permissions.

Apress titles may be purchased in bulk for academic, corporate, or promotional use. eBook versions and licenses are also available for most titles. For more information, reference our Print and eBook Bulk Sales web page at http://www.apress.com/bulk-sales.

Any source code or other supplementary material referenced by the author in this book is available to readers on GitHub via the book's product page, located at www.apress.com/978-1-4842-4887-4. For more detailed information, please visit http://www.apress.com/source-code.

Printed on acid-free paper

Table of Contents

About the Author

Charles Waghmare has been working at Capgemini since 2011 in various roles, such as Yammer community manager and global lead for the Enterprise Knowledge Management platform (known as KM3.0). In addition, he manages the development of Knowledge Management Portal built in SharePoint Online to host client references and knowledge assets related to artificial intelligence and customer experiences. Charles has been an active promoter of Microsoft Azure Chatbots to automate processes, develop engaging conversation with users, and create new use cases for Azure Chatbots.

Before joining Capgemini, Charles worked with ATOS (formerly SIEMENS Information Systems Ltd.) for five years. He was community manager of System Application Product-based communities at ATOS using Technoweb 2.0—a Yammer-like platform. He was also responsible for managing the Communities of Practice initiative. In addition, Charles was a global rollout manager for a structured document management system built in SharePoint on-premise.

About the Technical Reviewer

 **Arun Sharma** leads the cloud business at Paytm Cloud as general manager of Enterprise Cloud. He has vast experience in cloud technologies (e.g., Microsoft Azure, AWS, GSuite), Internet of Things, machine learning, Micro services, bots, Docker, and containerization. He has almost 17 years of experience in a wide variety of roles, such as delivery manager at Microsoft, product manager at Icertis, lead and architect associate at Infosys, executive trainer at Aptech, and development consultant at CMC. He managed relationship, sales, cloud consumption, and consulting services; and adoption with medium and large global customers.

Arun loves challenges in the Microsoft playing field, combining them with his domain knowledge in banking, insurance, fast-moving consuming goods, local government, retail, and telecom. He is very active in the community as an author of international research papers, technical speaker, reviewer, blog writer, and LinkedIn sales navigator. He also holds the title of certified trainer from Microsoft and is completing his doctorate in business administration. Arun Sharma can found on Twitter at @arunkhoj.

Acknowledgments

The fear of the LORD is the beginning of knowledge. —Proverbs 1:7
First of all, I offer honor and praise to my God, Lord Jesus Christ, who gives me opportunities to write books. I am grateful to my God, Lord Christ, and dedicate this book to Him and to His glory.

To my dearest parents, **Mr. David Genu Waghmare** and **Mrs. Kamla Waghmare**, for their eternal love, I thank them from the bottom of my heart for their care, encouragement, and motivation until this day. God bless you both. I thank my dearest sisters: **Usha, Esther, Margret, Diana, Carol, and Mary**. Especially, I appreciate the support of my sisters **Carol and Mary** in times of difficulty and pain. I thank my adorable nephews: **Kris**, who is passionate about fitness and has tremendous love for cats; and **Savio**, who appreciates a world of harmonium, tanpura, and classical music. I enjoy spending time with them. And, special thanks to my fiancé **Miss Priya Muniraj**, for creating a positive impact by coming into my life!

I offer the following thanks as well to **Miss Nisha Talwar**, Engagement Manager at Capgemini, for her continuous support and encouragement; to **Mr. Sreeprasad MK**, Team Manager at Capgemini, for his care; and to **Mr. Balkrishna Shirgaonker** and **Mrs. Reshma Kamath**, Senior Consultants at Capgemini, who jointly shouldered my burden during my difficult days. To **The Salvation Army Church**; Matunga Corps, Mumbai; and **Amazing Grace Assembly of God** Church, Bangalore; special thanks to all church members for your love and affection.

CHAPTER 1

Introduction: Azure Chatbots

In this introductory chapter, we take a simple, initial, and down-to-earth look at artificial intelligence (AI) and chatbots. We examine Azure and Azure chatbots, and, last, study how to build chatbots using Azure chatbots. Readers with technical backgrounds and nontechnical backgrounds can gain an understanding of chatbots. In general, if you are fond of technology, passionate about digital transformation, and have a desire to bring about change, generate user engagement, and create high impact in terms of customer satisfaction, then this book is for you.

Introduction to AI

AI is one of the hot topics in digital transformation. The entire world is investing huge amounts of money to build intelligent systems that can think and behave like humans, and engage humans in conversation to determine solutions to their problems. John McCarthy, the father of AI, defined it as: "The science and engineering of making intelligent machines, especially intelligent computer programs."

AI is the science through which we can develop intelligent robots controlled by computers, or software applications that think like humans and interact with them using human common sense. AI systems are built

© Charles Waghmare 2019
C. Waghmare, *Introducing Azure Bot Service*,
https://doi.org/10.1007/978-1-4842-4888-1_1

by studying thinking patterns of human beings and how people learn, make decisions, and work toward fixing problems. For example, a bot is an example of an AI-based system that was developed to engage humans in conversation. Think of a bot as a smart robot that interacts with people to provide answers to our questions.

AI Applications

So now we know that AI systems are smart systems that have been created based on studies of thinking and behavior patterns of human beings. Let's look at how AI has been used in different fields, such as gaming, natural language processing (NLP), expert systems, vision systems, intelligent robots, and IBM Watson.

Gaming

AI plays a big role in video games and is used primarily to determine the behavior of nonplayer characters in games and to define the way the computer opponent behaves. Popular video games such as Mario, chess, poker, and Road Rash use AI to create human experiences for gaming players.

Natural Language Processing

NLP refers to the AI method of communicating with an intelligent system by using a natural language used by humans, such as English. NLP is required when you want an intelligent system, such as a robot, to perform tasks based on your instructions and to retrieve useful information to assist you in making decisions. Inputs and outputs for NLP-based AI systems are written text and speech. One familiar example of an NLP-based AI system is Alexa.

Alexa was developed based on NLP, which involved procedures that converted speech into words, sounds, and ideas. When instructions in the form of sound are given by people, Amazon (the owner of Alexa), records the words, breaks the words into parts, and consults a database that contains various word pronunciations to determine which words correspond most closely to the combination of individual sounds. In addition, Alexa identifies keywords to make sense of the tasks and carries out corresponding functions per the instructions given. For instance, if Alexa notices words such as *jeans* or *T-shirt*, it opens a fashion app. Amazon's servers then send the information back to your device and Alexa describes the relevant information being sent. Entire conversations take place very quickly, with high-level computation time—the time it takes the information to be sent from a device to Amazon servers and vice versa.

Expert Systems

In AI, an expert system is a computer system that helps human beings make decisions based on inputs entered into it. Such systems are designed to solve complex problems by using existing knowledge in the system and with the help of defining rules, rather than using lists of conventional procedural code.

Expert systems are highly responsive, reliable, and understandable. Expert systems are used in medicine, science, engineering, and so on. The knowledge stored in expert systems is based on knowledge shared by people. Organizations run campaigns to increase the knowledge in expert systems. Today, there are smart enterprise search engines that consider not only keywords used for searches, but also user browsing behavior, profile information, and search trends to extract useful search results from expert systems.

Vision Systems

AI-based vision systems are used to understand, interpret, detect, and comprehend visual input entered into computer systems. For example, developed countries send aircraft to unexplored areas to take photographs that can be used to figure out spatial information or to map these areas. Medical doctors use these systems to aid in their diagnosis of patients based on visual patient inputs. Police use computer software to run facial recognition software to identify suspects based on stored portraits created by forensic artists.

Intelligent Robots

Intelligent robots are able to comprehend human input, process it, make decisions and choose thebest one, then offer it as output to human beings. They have sensors that detect physical data from the real world, such as temperature, light, heat, movement, sound, cushion, and pressure. They are equipped with efficient processors, multiple sensors, and a huge amount of memory so they can exhibit intelligence. In addition, they are capable of learning from their mistakes and can be made to adapt to new environments. A well-known example of intelligent robots is Alibaba, a famous Chinese online e-commerce web site used for delivering orders. The robots operate in a warehouse. When a product request is generated through Alibaba, the most idle robot receives the request, goes to the shelf where the product is located, takes the product off the shelf, then unloads it onto a packing tray for delivery to the customer. Huge warehouses are managed by multiple intelligent robots that operate within a defined time frame.

IBM Watson for Chatbots

We conclude this discussion of AI applications by examining IBM Watson, which is a question-and-answer supercomputer that works based on natural human language and was built using AI. Apart from NLP, this question-and-answer system was built using information retrieval, knowledge representation, automated reasoning, and machine learning technologies.

The main difference between a question-and-answer mechanism and a document search is that a document search takes a keyword query and returns a list of documents, ranked in order of relevance to the query (often based on popularity and page ranking), whereas question-and-answer technology takes a question expressed in natural human language, comprehends it in much greater detail, and provides output with a precise answer to the question.

With IBM Watson, organizations have built chatbots to serve customers 24/7 that meet their expectations and build customer satisfaction. With the AI built in IBM Watson, it has helped global teams discover answers to complex questions with speed and accuracy so these teams can focus on innovative and interesting work. For organizations working on contracts, Watson provides great assistance with contract governance by analyzing and comparing contract elements rapidly—such as obligations, clauses, rights, and parties—and flags differences within seconds. This capability makes searches very easy, regardless of whether exact terms are used.

The Current State of AI

Today, AI applications are not just limited to information technology (IT). They have extensive use in a variety of areas. Let's take a look at some of them.

Siri

Siri is one of the most iconic examples of a personal assistant offered by Apple with its iPhone and iPad. Siri has a built-in friendly voice that interacts with users on a daily basis. Siri assists users in finding information, getting directions, exchanging messages, making voice calls, opening applications, and adding events to calendars. It uses machine learning technology to act intelligently. Furthermore, it is capable of understanding natural language questions and requests. It is currently one of the greatest examples of the machine learning abilities of gadgets.

Tesla

If you are a technology geek and dream of owning a car like the ones shown in Hollywood movies, a Tesla is what you need in your garage. This car is getting smarter day by day through over-the-air updates. Automobiles are moving toward AI. Tesla is one of the best automobiles the world has produced, and has features such as self-driving and predictive capabilities.

Cogito

One of the best examples of a behavioral AI system is Cogito, which was cofounded by Sandy Pentland and Joshua Feast. Cogito was developed based on machine learning and behavioral science to enhance customer collaboration for phone professionals. Cogito handles millions of calls on a daily basis. The AI solution within it analyzes the human voice and provides real-time guidance to enhance behavior.

Netflix

Today, you watch films either in a movie theater or on Netflix, which is known around the world as a one-stop shop for movies. Netflix—a content on-demand service—uses predictive technology to offer recommendations based on user reactions such as interests, choices, and behavior. AI built into Netflix identifies records related to user reactions to recommend movies based on shows that you've watched previously. The only drawback to this technology is that small movies go unnoticed and big films grow and become famous.

Pandora

Pandora is one of the most popular and high-demand technology solutions for music lovers. It is also known as the DNA of music. Based on 400 musical characteristics, a team of expert musicians individually analyzed songs that were then shared with end users. This system also recommends other music that would otherwise never get noticed except for the reactions of other users.

Nest

Nest is an AI solution that uses behavioral algorithms to save energy based on user schedules and behaviors. It was a successful and quite famous AI startup that was acquired by Google in 2014 for $3.2 billion. It uses a machine learning process that considers consumers' body temperature, programs itself in a week, and regulates cooling or heating systems when consumers are not home. It uses a combination of both AI and Bluetooth low energy to provide the desired end results.

Boxever

Boxever is an AI solution that provides incredible experiences for travelers. It relies heavily on machine learning to enhance customer experiences and it makes travel recommendations to create memorable holidays.

Drones

Drones are based on a machine learning system that translates the environment into a three-dimensional model that uses sensors and video cameras. The sensors and camera are used to track the position of a drone, and a trajectory algorithm guides the drone on how and where to move. Drones are used for specific purposes, such as product delivery, news reporting, and discovery of unknown areas.

Echo

Echo was developed by Amazon. It is a revolutionary product that works like a search engine to help you find information on the Internet. It also schedules appointments, manages home lighting, answers questions based on information from the Internet, accesses and reads audio books aloud, and alerts users of traffic status and weather conditions. In addition, Echo notifies you of sports updates, business reviews, and job postings.

Types of AI

AI is gaining in popularity as a result of its wide use at a rapid pace. It has created a huge impact on people and the way we collaborate. AI will continue to bring innovative changes to our world, and will transform businesses and customer experiences. Of course, there are different types of AI. Let's take a look at some of them now.

Reactive Machines

A famous example of a reactive machine is IBM's chess-playing computer called Deep Blue, which defeated grandmaster chess player Garry Kasparov in the late 1990s.

Limited Memory

Limited-memory AI is used primarily in self-driving cars. Sensors detect constantly the movement of vehicles around them. Data such as lane markers, traffic lights, and curves in the road will be added to AI machines to prevent cars from getting hit by nearby vehicles. It takes less than 100 seconds for an AI system to make decisions while self-driving.

Theory of Mind

Theory of mind is an advanced technology that is able to understand people's emotions, beliefs, thoughts, and expectations, and can interact socially. Plenty of improvements are needed in this field. This kind of AI is not complete yet.

Self-aware

Self-aware AI has its own consciousness, is superintelligent, has self-awareness and sentient, and is, quite simply, a complete human being. In reality, this kind of chatbot does not currently exist and, if achieved, will be a milestone in the field of AI.

Artificial Narrow Intelligence

Artificial narrow intelligence (ANI) is found in smartphones like Cortana and Siri, and helps users to respond to their problems on request. This type of AI is referred to as *weak AI* or *narrow AI* because it focuses on one task, as opposed strong AI, which focuses on multiple tasks. Siri operates within limited, predefined ranges of function and hence it is an example of ANI.

Artificial General Intelligence

The Pillo robot is an example of artificial general intelligence that answers questions regarding the health of family members. It distributes medication and provides guidance for improving health. This is powerful technology, which is necessary for those requiring full-time healthcare.

Artificial Superhuman Intelligence

Artificial superhuman intelligence achieves everything a human can do and more. Alpha 2 is the first humanoid robot developed for the family that can manage a smart home and things in your home. It also provides updates of nearby weather conditions and tells you interesting stories.

Chatbots: An Introduction

A chatbot is a virtual entity loaded with knowledge, which is shared in the form of output when a human being performs a chat, which can be casual or formal. Sometimes chatbots are powered with machine learning, so they can act smarter based on their interactions and provide relevant answers to questions asked by users. Information is loaded in the form of a question and an answer. When the chabot receives a question, it knows the answer as well. Chatbots enabled with AI store human interactions in the form of personas and reuse existing personas to provide intelligent solutions.

Examples of chatbots include Facebook Messenger, Siri, WeChat, Telegram, SMS, Slack, Skype, and many others. Popular chatbots such as Alexa, which function using voice communication, are currently quite popular.

History of Chatbots

The idea of chatbots was conceived by Alan Turing and Joseph Weizenbaum. These two men imagined computers communicating like humans and, in 1950, developed the Turing test to determine whether a person could distinguish a human from a machine. In 1966, a computer program called ELIZA was invented by Weizenbaum. It imitated the language of a psychotherapist using two hundred lines of code. Check out `http://psych.fullerton.edu/mbirnbaum/psych101/Eliza.htm` to create your own conversation. Sample dialog is provided here:

> Psychotherapist (chatbot): I am a psychotherapist. Please tell me your problem.
>
> Patient (human being): I have terrible headache.
>
> Psychotherapist: You should consult a doctor. I am a psychotherapist.
>
> Patient: I will try. Can you elaborate?
>
> Psychotherapist: No, I cannot understand. See you later.
>
> Patient: You are talking nonsense. I will talk to a doctor myself.

The first move away from text chatbots to a voice-operated entertainment AI chatbot occurred in 1988, when Rollo Carpenter started the Jabberwocky Project.

In 2000, Robert Hoffer from ActiveBuddy Inc. cocreated the SmarterChild chatbot that used AOL Instant Messenger and MSN Messenger to build a relationship with more than 30 million users. The chatbot provided access to news, weather, and movie times, and acted as a personal assistant using natural language comprehension.

With recent developments in technology, chatbots have become even more powerful in interpreting natural language and machine learning to understand users better and learn over time. Huge companies such as Facebook, Apple, Google, and Microsoft are spending significant money delivering interactions between consumers and machines with commercially viable business models.

Chatbots deliver multiple services. They can check the weather forecast or be used to purchase a new pair of shoes—and anything in between. They can help you book your travel tickets, choose the best pizza in your neighborhood, and shop for clothes. Currently, consumers are spending more time using messaging applications than social media, and messaging applications are now the most popular way companies deliver chatbot experiences to consumers.

In general, there are two types of chatbots. One type follows a set of defined rules, flows, and triggers to respond to very specific commands provided by users. A simple example is a chatbot that tells you the traffic status of a particular road. A user might ask, "How is the traffic on Highway 287?" The chatbot determines the answer and responds. The success of this type of chatbot is contingent on the intelligence of the developers who created it by covering each and every context of a situational conversation.

The other type of chatbot depends on using machine learning to try to understand the sentiment and meaning of the language used. It does not rely on preplanned sets of commands created by developers. A user might ask, "What's happening in FIFA World Cup matches?" The chatbot might deliver resources that provide the latest scores and updates from the most current FIFA matches. This type of chatbot learns from conversations to improve accuracy and understanding over time. The following is a list of companies that currently use chatbots:

- Uber and Lyft to book a ride

- Airlines such as Air France and Qantas Airways to deliver precise flight information

- Media companies such as the BBC and CNN to keep you up to date with news

- Business web sites such as TechCrunch to keep you up to date with techie content

- Food chains such as Pizza Hut, Dominos, KFC, MacDonald's, and Wendy's to order food

- Cosmetic companies such as Sephora and L'Oréal to provide beauty tips and a shopping experience

- Banks such as BNP Paribas, Bank of America, and Wells Fargo to connect customers to their finances

- Pharmacies such as Walgreens and Publix to provide information on medication

- Supermarkets such as Walmart and Kroger for consumers to order groceries

Chatbots in Action

Imagine you are driving and suddenly crave a cup of coffee. Because you are driving, you cannot text, but you remember that a coffee chatbot is installed on your mobile phone that understands your voice and can help you hunt for the nearest coffee shop. Here is an example of a conversation you might have:

> You: Good morning. Can you help me find a good place to get coffee near me?
>
> Search chatbot: There are three coffee shops near you that have five-star consumer ratings.
>
> You: Please add the highest rated coffee shop chatbot to this chat.
>
> Coffee chatbot: Hello, sir. This is coffee bot.
>
> You: Please send directions to your shop and place an order for a regular cappuccino and two croissants.

Coffee chatbot: Directions have been added to your map. Do you want to pay using your wallet?

You: Yes

Coffee chatbot: OK. Five dollars has been paid. The receipt will be sent to your e-mail address.

Chatbot: Sir, I've noticed that you have a client meeting in Lawrenceville, which is about 30 miles away from the coffee shop. Would you like me to send you the fastest route so you can reach your destination in time?

You: Yes, please.

Chatbot: Directions have been added to your map.

You: Oh no! My car just broke down. Please book me a ride so I can get to my meeting in time.

Chatbot: A ride has been booked and the details have been added to our conversation. Would you like me to find a service provider who has five-star services to help repair your car?

You: Yes. Please send the current car location and owner details to the service provider so they can fix my car and deliver it to my house.

Chatbot: Done, sir.

You: Thank you.

Chatbot: Have a good rest of the day, sir.

Before 2015, everyone used to say, "There's an app for everything." At that time, every business focused on mobile app development; apps became part of corporate fundamental business strategies.

With the evolution of Chatbots, things have changed; companies experience greater returns on investments compared to apps. Platforms that enable the delivery of chatbot experiences are available to more consumers, and more innovative ways are being adopted to create greater returns on investments and develop continuous user interaction to transform business tractions to effect business growth.

Introducing Azure

Azure was introduced by Microsoft in 2008 as Windows Azure. Its name has since been changed to Microsoft Azure. Its service platform provides space for host software, which is done in the form of virtual machines (VMs). You can choose whichever operating system you want, whichever database you want, and the front-end technology required to host your data. This entire process takes a few brief minutes. The following list contains an overview of the services provided by Azure:

- *Compute:* Includes VMs, functions for serverless computing, batches for containerized batch workloads, service fabric for microservices, container orchestration, and cloud services to build cloud-based apps and application programming interfaces (APIs)

- *Networking:* Provides numerous networking tools such as Virtual Network (which can connect to on-premise data centers) load balancer, Application Gateway, VPN Gateway, Azure DNS for domain hosting, Content Delivery Network, Traffic Manager, ExpressRoute dedicated private network fiber connections, and Network Watcher monitoring and diagnostics

- *Storage:* Enables file and disk storage, with backup and disaster recovery provision

- *Web and mobile:* Provides all services to create and deploy web and mobile applications

- *Containers:* Includes Container Service (which supports Kubernetes, DC/OS, or Docker Swarm) and Container Registry, as well as tools for microservices

- *Databases:* Includes several SQL-based databases and related tools

- *Analytics:* Includes HDInsight for Hadoop Spark, R Server, HBase, and Storm clusters

- *AI and cognitive services:* Enables AI application development and provides capabilities such as computer vision APIs, face APIs, Bing web search, video indexer, and language understanding intelligence

- *Internet of Things (IoT):* IoT is the interconnection through the Internet of computing devices embedded in everyday objects, enabling them to send and receive data. Azure provides IoT Hub and IoT Edge services, which are combined with a variety of machine learning, analytics, and communications services.

- *Security and identity:* Includes Security Center, Azure Active Directory, and multifactor authentication services

- *Developer tools:* Includes development services such as Visual Studio Team Services, Azure DevTest Labs, HockeyApp mobile app deployment and monitoring, Xamarin cross-platform mobile development, and more

Azure helps businesses transform their operations with its cloud computing services. Here are some advantages of Microsoft Azure:

- *No capital investment:* Organizations need not worry about high infrastructure management costs because Azure cuts out the high cost of hardware. With its pay-as-you-go, subscription-based payment model, costs are easy to manage. To create an account in Azure, you simply register in Azure Portal and select your subscription based on your business needs.

- *Less operational costs:* Azure has a low operational cost because it runs on its own servers hosted in its own data centers. With a service-level agreement (SLA) of 100% availability for the services it provides, Azure is usually a whole lot more reliable than your own on-location server. If you were to set up your own server, you would need to hire a tech support team to monitor it and make sure things run smoothly. Also, there may be situations when the tech support team takes too much time to solve server issues. Microsoft Azure takes care of server monitoring, with tools and a dedicated internal team, without additional costs to your business.

- *Easy backup and disaster recovery options:* Azure keeps backups of all your valuable data with a perfect backup strategy. It has tried-and-tested disaster recovery procedures. In the event of a loss of data, you can recover it all with a single click, without affecting your business. Cloud-based backup and recovery solutions save time and money. Your organization does not need to make huge investments in backup, storage, and disaster management.

17

- *Easy to implement:* It is very simple to implement your business models in Azure. With just a few clicks, you are good to go. Microsoft provides tutorials to facilitate learning and deployment.

- *Better security:* Azure has strong security standards that are recognized internationally (such as IS27001 and SAS70) and the infrastructure gets audited on a regular basis. Business application and business-critical data are always secure with Azure.

- *Work from anywhere:* Azure gives you the freedom to work from anywhere. It requires an Internet connection and credentials. And with Azure cloud services offering mobile apps, you're not restricted to using a computer.

- *Increased collaboration:* With Azure, teams in various geographic locations and different time zones can access, edit, and share documents anytime, from anywhere. They can work collaboratively to achieve future goals. Azure preserves records of activity. Timestamps are one example of Azure's record keeping. They improve team collaboration by establishing transparency and increasing accountability.

Building a Chatbot Using Azure Bot Services

We have now come to the final part of this chapter, where we see how to build a chatbot using Azure Portal. As we have seen in this chapter so far, chatbots are becoming popular because they allow customers to interact in a conversational way. E-mail has become cluttered because people need information faster. Chatbots help consumers find solutions without using any forms, e-mail verification, or phone verification, and consumers are happy because they feel they have been attended to personally by a human being in the background. Let's now build a chatbot in minutes using Azure Portal.

QnA Maker is a free, easy-to-use web-based service available in Azure Portal that trains AI to respond to questions in a natural, conversational way. This service is compatible across development platforms, hosting services and channels, and it is a unique question-and-answer service with a graphical user interface. You do not have to be a developer to build and deploy in minutes a question-and-answer bot based on frequently asked questions (FAQs), URLs, structured documents, or editorial content.

Building the Chatbot

The following instructions show you how to build a chatbot using QnA Maker and then make it visible as a "web chat" channel with which anyone can communicate online.

1. Go to Azure Portal and make sure you need a subscription. From Azure Marketplace, click Create a resource, then click AI + Machine Learning, and then Web App Bot (Figure 1-1).

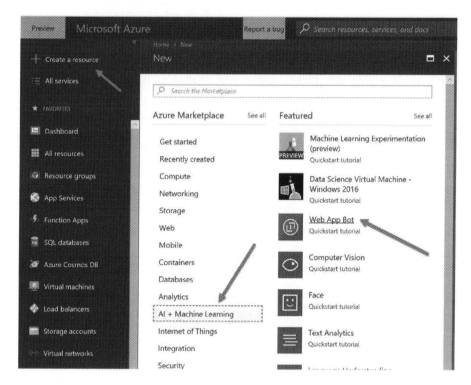

Figure 1-1. *Creating a resource in Azure Portal*

2. After the resource is created, in the Web App Bot screen, add a unique name for your bot. Mandatory values are prepopulated, but you can edit them. Then, click Bot template and select Question and Answer as the template. Last, click Select (Figure 1-2).

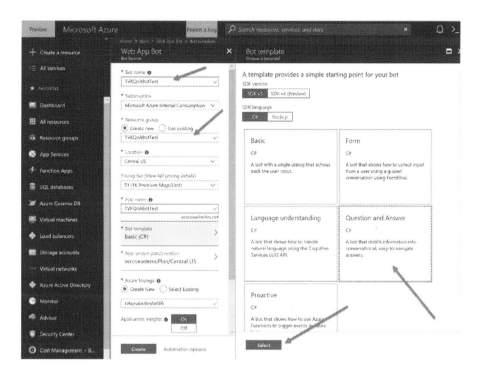

Figure 1-2. *Naming your chatbot*

3. After you have selected the Question and Answer
   template, click Create to create the chatbot
   (Figure 1-3).

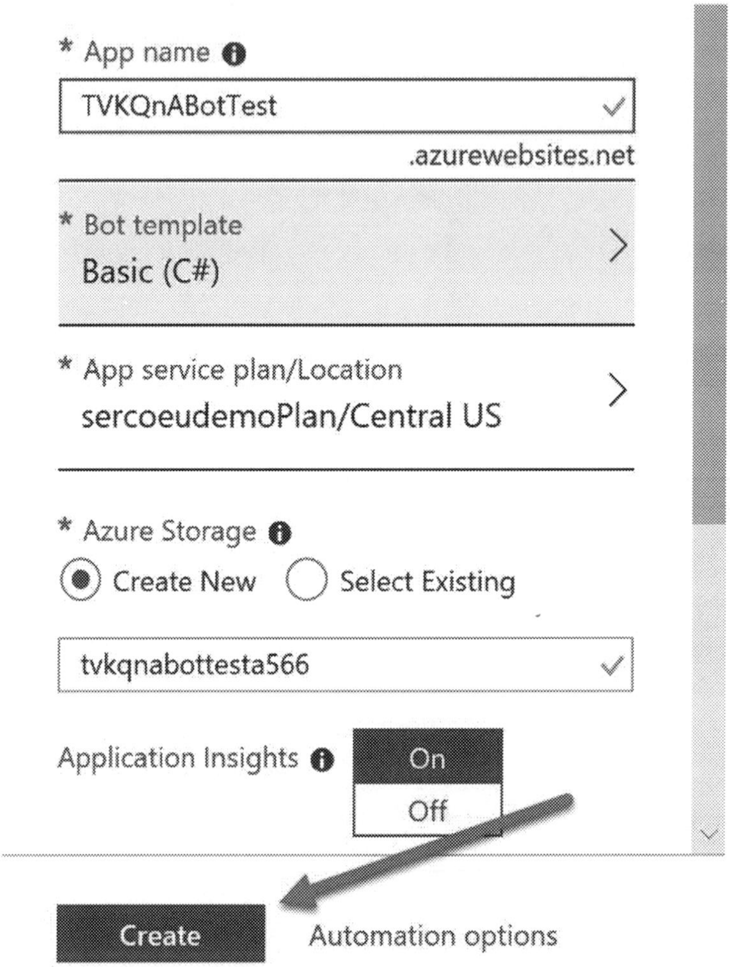

Figure 1-3. *Creating a chatbot*

Creating the Question-and-Answer Service

Your chatbot is now created and deployed. Now we need to create the question-and-answer service by taking the following steps:

1. Log in to QnA Maker using https://www.qnamaker.ai/. After logging in, click Create a knowledge base to create a question-and-answer service.

2. From the knowledge base screen, click Create a QnA service (Figure 1-4). The software redirects you to Azure Portal to update details on the new question-and-answer service. Post this, and deployment of the question-and-answer service occurs.

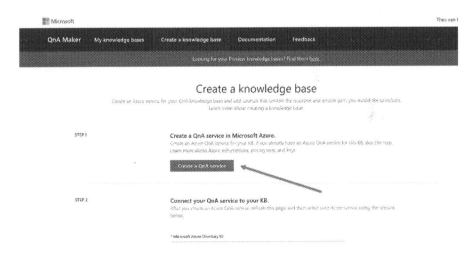

Figure 1-4. *Creating a cognitive question-and-answer service*

3. Figure 1-5 shows the values to use.

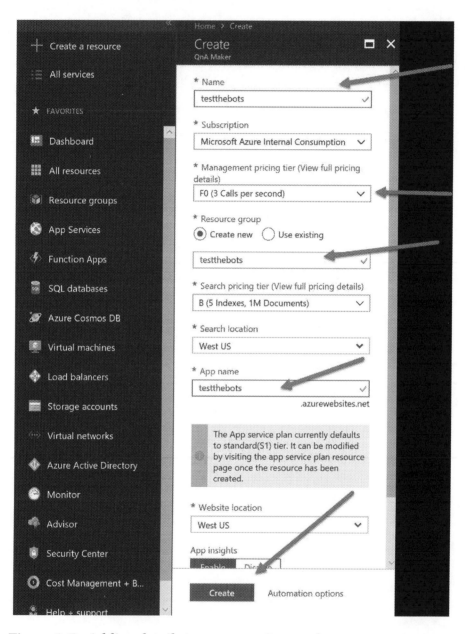

Figure 1-5. *Adding details to your question-and-answer service in Azure Portal*

4. From the Create knowledge base page, do the following:

- Give your question-and-answer service a name (Figure 1-6).

- Add the URL of a FAQ site you want to prowl for questions and answers. There is also an option to upload a file if you do not want to have a FAQ site (Figures 1-6 and 1-7).

- Click Create your KB (Figure 1-6).

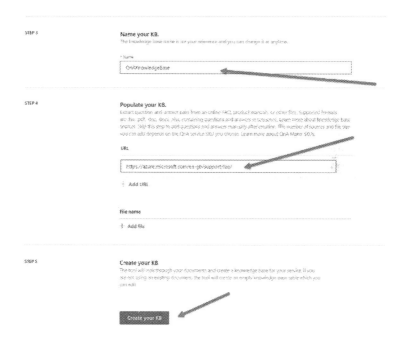

Figure 1-6. *Creating the knowledge base*

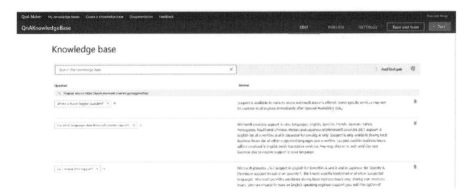

Figure 1-7. *Building FAQs*

5. Set up the FAQs that will be asked by your users.

6. After you publish your FAQs, you need to provide three values—QnAKnowledgebaseId, QnAEndpointHostName, and QnAAuthKey (Figure 1-8)—for the question-and-answer service to be configured as a chatbot.

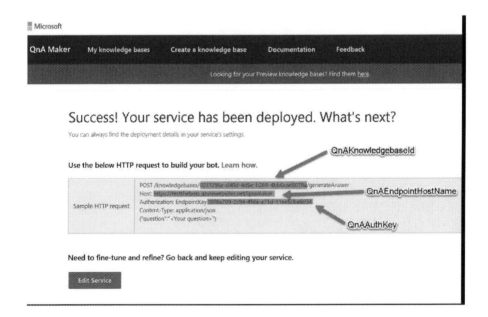

Figure 1-8. *Authorization keys*

7. Go to the resource page of your created chatbot
    and, under Application Settings, update
    QnAKnowledgebaseId, QnAEndpointHostName, and
    QnAAuthKey, then click Save (Figure 1-9).

Figure 1-9. *Configuring the authorization keys*

8. A web app chatbot is normally deployed as a web
    chat channel automatically, but you can also
    deploy to other channels, such as Skype, Cortana,
    Slack, Facebook Messenger, Bing, and more. Go to
    Channels and click "Get bot embed codes." Copy
    and paste the embedded code in your web site
    where you would to deploy your chatbot.

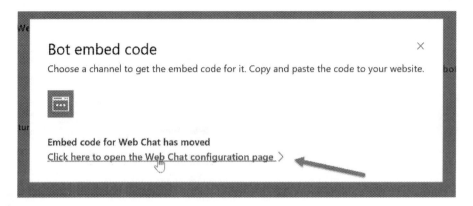

Figure 1-10. *Embedding the chatbot code*

9. From the Configuration page, click Show to check
    out one of the secret keys (either will do). Copy
    the contents of the "Embed code" text box to
    somewhere else and replace YOUR_SECRET_HERE
    with the secret key (Figure 1-11).

Figure 1-11. *Secret keys*

Your chatbot is now configured successfully on your web site. The chatbot can be accessed through the web site, a mobile app, or popular communications apps such as Facebook Messenger, Slack, Kik, and others.

Summary

In this chapter, we explored AI and different types of AI systems. In addition, we examined chatbots and Azure. Last, we went through a practical illustration of how conversational chatbots can be created from Azure Portal. In the next chapter, we learn about the Microsoft Bot Framework and the workings of a chatbot using an example from the retail industry to demonstrate how chatbots have helped to overcome challenges in retail.

CHAPTER 2

Deploy Chatbots in Your Business

This chapter is dedicated to different business scenarios in which chatbots can be implemented to gain business benefits. In this chapter, we look at various business challenges that can be resolved by implementing chatbots and then we examine the benefits of chatbots. Last, we see how chatbots enhance the customer experience.

Traditional Business Scenario

Today, businesses have become very dynamic, and the customer experience itself is a big challenge for organizations because of competition in the marketplace. Let's look at some examples of challenges in the retail industry. End user demands are so high there is no room for compromise. Consumers demand products of their choice, at discounted rates and packed with multiple offers and cash back, and ask that these products be delivered to their home for free as quickly as possible. These products are purchased online while consumers sit at home. Some consumers are bored with visiting standalone grocery stores. They prefer to visit a mall, where they can buy groceries, then watch a movie, and dine at a restaurant. Other consumers order their food and groceries online while sitting at home. Consumers buy home appliances, such as refrigerators and washing machines, online. They buy clothes, electronics, groceries, medication, and furniture online. The retail industry is transforming constantly as a result of increased customer demand and the desire to meet customer expectations. In addition, the retail industry faces challenges such as cost reduction, operations efficiency, customer expectations and experience, human resources, and inflation. Customers are more demanding and there is always extra pressure to exceed their expectations in products, services, and buying experiences.

There have been quite a lot of retail bankruptcies, but also there are many major retailers that have managed to survive and grow their businesses around the world. They have proved themselves to be Best in Class and are able to face major challenges within their respective industries. The following sections detail some common challenges faced by the retail industry. However, some of them have been mitigated by implementing AI solutions such as chatbots.

Managing Ever-changing Customer Expectations

Customer preferences are always bound to change, and most of the time they do so faster than the speed of a bullet train. Customer preferences depend on personal choices, seasonal trends, choices recommended by families and friends, and available offers. Thus, it is very important for retail businesses to engage customers, understand their expectations, and fulfil their expectations. Normally, retailers do not change products every day, but they do offer different elements such as discounts on and offers for products based on customer trends and demand. In short, retail businesses need to innovate every day.

Chatbots can help manage the majority of customer expectations. The most challenging thing is to understand customer need and offer affordable products without losing the consumer. During this entire process, customer engagement is important. But, if a customer is virtual, it becomes more difficult because there is no "look and feel" of a product from the customer's point of view. Engaging customers through chatbots means you must understand their demands, offer the right products, and generate the look and feel of products with images. These customer engagements are recorded by chatbots and the results are aggregated in the form of customer trends to make product-based decisions and future plans. This information is then used as the basis for offering additional products to customers per current trends.

Preserve Customer Loyalty

Customer loyalty is one important aspect of business growth, and the loyalty factor is related to the customer experience. If you make customers think they can be easily replaced, retailers will find it difficult to survive. By receiving an exceptional customer experience, the same customers will visit your shop again and again to purchase items online or in person. Most important, they share their experiences with others.

Promotions and offers are not the way to retain customers. Personalization has now become an important factor. To be in touch with your customers personally, you need to connect with them at a personal level. However, this is close to impossible without the help of staff. Chatbots have taken personalization to the next level—above personal e-mails and text messages—and have created a bond between customers and businesses. With chatbots, retailers can connect personally with their customers, ask what they need or what new items they want, update them about products and offers, and send surprise gifts. With chatbots, interactions with customers coexist as communication between two human beings.

Build an Employee Bond for an Effective Customer Experience

With complex customer demands, managing staff has become challenging for retail organizations. This challenge is faced mainly by large-scale retail companies that have multiple locations, but they are unable to communicate and collaborate with their employees, which can disrupt business processes. Retail organizations do not understand that their employees are their own customers, and they need to develop similar customers.

With the internal implementation of chatbots, retail organizations collect employee feedback and deploy training programs, among many others. Interactions captured by chatbots are again aggregated into trends and patterns to find scopes for new opportunities.

Employee Retention

The retail industry is one that has the highest employee attrition. Employee retention is one of the toughest challenges in industry. And hiring employees requires a lot of energy and operational costs.

Chatbots are an effective solution to this challenge. They are used to increase employee engagement with the company. Using chatbots, a business can suggest training programs for employee growth and acquisition of skills. Organizations have deployed human resource assistance with chatbots that offer help and services with regard to employee benefits, medical claims, leave management, and transport facilities.

Rapid Growth of Digital Customers

In this era of digital transformation, consumer behavior changes rapidly. With the rapid growth of e-commerce, consumers have ample choices when purchasing products. Although some consumers prefer buying products online, there are traditional consumers who still love to buy products in stores. They access the Internet to read product features and reviews, but they like to go to the store to make a purchase.

Nowadays, touch screens are installed to capture customer interactions for those consumers who buy products in stores. Touch screens contain chatbots and provide offline access to the store. Big retailers such Walmart and Kroger have installed chatbots in their huge stores for product recommendations, product location within the store, registration for loyalty programs, and for billing as self-service.

So far, we have seen how challenges in retail can be overcome by using chatbots, which help primarily by engaging with consumers to provide product recommendations, offers, and discount information; to address employee queries; and provide self-service checkout, thereby generating customer loyalty and an enhanced customer experience.

A study by Oracle (documented by Business Insider), predicted that 80% of businesses reported they already use or plan to use chatbots by 2020. According to figures available on the emarketer web site, 1.4 billion people a year are now interacting with chatbots. In general, chatbots live inside apps such as Facebook Messenger, Internet web sites, and e-mail applications. In a formal, conversational way, they converse with customers to execute a number of tasks, from ordering items to suggesting and finding products. The following sections provide examples of innovative companies that have deployed chatbots successfully to help improve operations, connect with customers, and increase sales.

1-800-Flowers

1-800-Flowers.com, Inc., is a floral and gourmet food gift retail organization and distribution company in the United States. It was one of the first retail organizations in the United States to use a 24/7 toll-free telephone number, then switched to the Internet to accept customer orders, and then finally switched to conversational commerce using chatbots to engage with customers.

1-800-Flowers.com uses a chatbot in Facebook Messenger to help customers send flowers to their dear ones directly from the bot instead of going through the company web site, which also serves as an online store. The bot offers recommendation on the type of flowers based on inputs provided by the customer. Furthermore, it helps customers update delivery addresses and make payments, provides offers and discount information, and provides timely updates on delivery. The bot also helps customers choose the message to be printed on the gift card sent with the flowers.

Sephora

Sephora is a French-based multinational chain of personal care and beauty stores that was established in Paris in 1970. Sephora offers about 300 brands, along with its own private label: Sephora. It is a world-class chain that offers beauty products, including cosmetics, skincare, fragrances, nail color, and haircare.

What is the lipstick worn by the Oscar winner? What is trending in nail color? Which lipstick will look good on me? Can I get a world-class perfume? Which nail color suits my skin tone? Which shampoo will give me silky hair? Answers to these questions are provided by chatbots within a few seconds. You can upload your picture to a virtual artist app and check out different looks. According to Sephora, more than 4 million people have used the chatbot and virtual artist app.

H&M

H&M is a multinational Swedish clothing company well known for its fashionable clothing for men, women, teenagers, and children. H&M has more than 4,500 stores in more than 62 countries and employs around 132,000 people.

H&M's chatbot quizzes customers about their style preferences, colors, size, trend, and fabric type. Based on this information, recommendations are made to customers based on their preferences. Customers can also select the type of clothes they want and, after making their final selection, the chatbot adds them to their cart and requests payment. This service is available for both online and offline shopping.

Disney

Disney has proved that chatbots are not limited to customer service, employee engagement, and sales. Chatbots can also be leveraged for strategic marketing initiatives, such as creating excitement for the release of its *Zootopia* film. To do so, Disney created an Officer Judy Hopps bot on Facebook Messenger to engage customers. This officer was one of the characters in the film.

On average, Disney found more than ten minutes were spent by users chatting with Officer Judy Hopps. This was an awesome experience—to be able to chat with Officer Judy before watching the film.

Casper

Casper Sleep is a United States-based e-commerce company that sells sleep products online. The company also has showrooms in New York City, San Francisco, and Los Angeles.

Casper's chatbot helps customers choose a mattress based on the size of the bed, color, and type of mattress. Interestingly, their chatbot is available during the night—between 11 p.m. and 5 a.m. The company believes there are some nights when people can't fall sleep and need Casper during the night, which is the reason for the bot to be operational during the night.

Why Do Businesses Need Chatbots?

In this section, we explore several reasons why today's businesses need chatbots to be successful. There is a tremendous increase in the number of users of messaging apps such as WhatsApp, Slack, and Skype, and Facebook Messenger alone has more than 1.2 million monthly users. Like messaging apps, virtual chatbots can imitate human conversation to help solve business problems and they have an increasing demand in the market. Chatbots are used to schedule a ride, order food, book a hotel and flight, make a doctor's appointment, and more. Stats used in this section are available from `chatbotsmagazine.com`.

Chatbots help in saving time and effort by automating customer support. Gartner has predicted that by 2020, more than 85% of customer interactions will be handled without human assistance. Chatbots not only handle customer inquiries, but also perform business tasks such as collecting customer information, scheduling meetings, and setting up conference calls, thereby reducing operational costs. The market of chatbots is on the rise, but, chatbots have not replaced couriers, doctors, and writers, for example.

Consumers also benefit from chatbots, and they are becoming more interested in using this technology. The results of a study were presented during the 4th International Conference on Internet Science in November 2017. The authors identified the major reasons why people choose to interact with chatbots. According to their research, the main factors that motivate people to use chatbots are as follows:

- *Entertainment:* Chatbots amuse people by giving them funny tips, and they act as a friend with consumers through engaging conversation.

- *Productivity:* Chatbots aid in finding and provide access to information quickly and efficiently when requested by consumers.

- *Curiosity:* People have developed an understanding of chatbots, and want to explore their abilities and try something new to enhance their customer experience.

- *Social and relational factors:* Chatbots fuel conversations and enhance social experiences. Chatting with bots also helps avoid loneliness and gives people a chance to talk without being judged. They also improve individual conversational skills.

Now let's look at some primary reasons why your business needs chatbots.

Scale up Your Operation

Chatbots do not have limitations like humans. Human agents can handle only two to three conversations at a time, with minimal accuracy. However, chatbots can operate without an upper limit and with accuracy. By deploying chatbot solutions to complement your human task force, your business can grow and survive in competitive markets.

Address High-volume Queries from Your Customers

If your business receives a lot of inquiries from customers, chatbots can take the pressure off your customer support team by handling multiple queries 24/7. As the first point of contact, chatbots can screen calls from customers and redirect them to human consultants when needed.

Recommend Products

With regard to Business-to-Business-to-Consumer (B2B2C), such as Amazon, when the same product is offered and sold by multiple companies, customers need recommendations for choosing their products. Chatbots help customers choose products based on the information they provide during their conversation. For example, what if you want to buy a cell phone and there are multiple options available, and each varies in terms of cost, features, availability, and ratings? A chatbot would help you make the decision to buy the right product for you.

Handle Gen Y Customers

Gen Y or millennial customers are not very easy to handle because they prefer to inquire and compare products before they decide to buy. Also, they prefer to chat using their smartphones, rather than speak to an actual human after waiting in a long queue. If you design products for Gen Y consumers, then investing in a chatbot is a must to enhance the customer experience and increase sales.

Maximize Personalization

The more you are in touch with your customers, the more business you are likely to get from them. You can send them e-mail, but they may not necessarily read it, and the same goes with Short Messaging Services (SMS). If you call them, they may get irritated. But, build a conversation with them using chatbots and they are likely to respond. Some banks have deployed chatbots to calculate consumer eligibility for personal, business, or home loans. The chatbot asks for information systematically and consumers are given a loan amount in a few seconds. Previously, human agents took days and months to calculate loan amounts.

A chatbot is designed to answer specific questions, instead of displaying vast amounts of information. Paying maximal attention to a customer increases the chance for your product to be purchased by the customer.

Create an Interactive Marketing Platform

Using web sites or cell phones to engage customers provides a passive customer experience. There is no personal touch with consumers. In the case of creating a marketing campaign, it is very difficult to reach consumers because the campaign traffic is unidirectional: from the business to the consumer. With chatbots, however, campaign traffic can travel in two directions, which helps to calculate the return on investment of the campaign.

Drive Organizational Efficiency

Chatbot deployment helps you manage your staff in the most effective manner. Your employees may not like to perform mundane or repetitive tasks day in and day out. They may prefer change and challenging work. Chatbots help by tackling repetitive tasks and providing 24/7 support effectively.

Product and services companies understand the benefits of using chatbots in daily operations, internal and external communication, employee engagement, and feedback acquisition from both employees and clients. Chatbots help to improve customer service and they are the best option for those business organizations that don't want their clients to go through a bad experience such as the following:

- Waiting for an operator to respond when your customer dials in: "Your call is very important to us. Please stay on the line." This is quite annoying.

- Having a customer search your FAQs page, which is more than 100 pages long

41

Chatbots help with the shopping process. They ask consumers pointed questions about the product they want to buy. The bot sends the information to the sales department and determines whether the product is available for purchase. If it is unavailable, the chatbot will tell the customer when the product will be available. Customers do not have to repeat their requests; the chatbot remembers the customer's preferences and uses this information when the customer returns.

Improve Response Rate

About 90% of questions sent from a company's Facebook business page remain unanswered. A chatbot guarantees a 100% response rate to questions and converts these leads into opportunities.

Automate Repetitive Tasks

Most customers expect to get answers for the same questions: What are your hours? Where are you located? Do you make deliveries in my area? Chatbots reduce the pain of answering duplicate questions by consumers.

Chatbot Design Considerations

The following are some design elements to consider when building a chatbot:

- *Define goals:* Determine why you want to create a chatbot. List the functions your chatbot needs to perform during customer interactions.

- *Choose a channel:* Determine where your chatbot will live. Host your chatbot per client preference for communication, whether it be a web site, mobile app, Facebook Messenger, WhatsApp, or other messaging platform.

- *Choose the development method:* Determine how you want to develop your chatbot: using ready-made chatbot functionality (which is available in Azure) or building a custom bot from scratch.

- *Create, customize, and launch:* Prepare questions the chatbot will answer and build in the answers the chatbot will deliver during conversations with customers. Double-check everything before rolling out the bot to production.

The main challenge in designing a chatbot is understanding the language of your customers. In every business, customers are bound to express themselves differently, may create typos during the conversation, and may have their own way of writing. Language depends on several factors, such advertising campaigns in the market, the political situation in a given country, and releases of new services and products from Google, Apple, and Pepsi, among others. The way people talk depends on factors such as location, mood, weather, and moon phase. Therefore, it is important to train a chatbot to understand correctly everything the consumer asks. This requires a lot of effort.

WeChat and Facebook: Two Famous Chatbots

Questions that business owners think about are: Aside from investing in web site development and a friendly mobile app, why would we invest in chatbots? Won't they put my organization at risk—with customers interacting with bots and not human beings? For conservative organizations that have always believed that customer loyalty is the human connection, not bots, for them this is the biggest step toward business transformation. Banking and insurance domains, which rely on human brains because they deal with money, most often think the switch to chatbots for customer service is a big risk initially. But, AI is the present and the future for businesses, and chatbots are an example of AI. To understand more, let's take a look at Facebook Messenger and WeChat— two organizations that deployed a chatbot solution well before other businesses to increase sales and engage customers more effectively.

WeChat

WeChat is a Chinese multipurpose mobile app used extensively in China for messaging, social media engagement, and mobile payment, and it was developed by an organization called Tencent. It was launched in 2011. By 2018, it was one of the world's largest standalone mobile apps by monthly active users, with more than 1 billion monthly active users. WeChat gained popularity across the globe as a result of its attractive stickers and its investment in chatbots. WeChat not only uses a text medium, but also voice recognition integrated with AI, which allows apps to do more challenging tasks than simple chatting. One of the core successes of chatbots is that users don't have to download a new app every time they need a new service.

The chatbot running on WeChat has been categorized into two segments: subscription accounts and service accounts. WeChat continues to focus on enhancing services offered by chatbots to create best-in-class customer experiences. The future development of chatbots includes increasing complexity and sophistication in currently operational chatbots so they can carry on long and meaningful conversations with end users and not act simply on FAQ-based strings of text sent by the user. WeChat has the most popular bot deployed on this platform, called Microsoft Xiaoice, with 40 million users in Japan and China. In addition, the voice of the bot can be changed based on signals it receives from users.

Facebook Messenger

Facebook Messenger is a chat application developed originally as Facebook Chat in 2008. Facebook revamped its messaging service in 2010, and subsequently released standalone iOS and Android apps in later years. Facebook has ambitions similar to WeChat and, by taking a leaf from the book of WeChat, Mark Zuckerberg, the chief executive officer of Facebook, developed an ambitious vision to turn the Facebook Messenger app into a commercial hub with the development and incorporation of multiple functionalities and utilities in a single app. It started with an integrated peer-to-peer payment method on the Messenger app, which then developed into a full-fledged chatbot API to interact with customers.

Facebook Messenger has more than 11,000 active chatbots and more than 23,000 registered accounts on wit.ai, Facebook's NLP service for developers. By making an ambitious move in the development of chatbots, Facebook has now integrated features such as sending responses in audio and video, as GIFs, and so on, in addition to text responses. This has increased sales and enhanced customer experiences of several big brands such as Sephora, whose Reservation Assistant chatbot has increased the average spent by a user by $50; SnapTravel's bot has seen bookings of more than $1 million in a year.

As a big, medium, or small company, if you are late to join the chatbot revolution, it is not too late to create best-in-class customer experiences. This is the right time to start investing in chatbots for your business.

Businesses Need a Chatbot, Not an App

In this section, we focus on a chatbot and mobile app comparison based on user experience and business trends, and determine which is important for current and future generations. The chatbot trend started in 2016, and some said that chatbots were the next web sites and apps. Businesses adopted more and more chatbots to do their job efficiently and gain profits. According to Internet trend reports published in 2016 (Table 2-1), average global users have 33 apps, of which 12 are used daily, with 80% of their time spent using three apps.

Table 2-1. *App Use*

Region	Average no. of apps installed on devices	Average no. of apps used daily	Average no. of apps accounting for 80% usage	Time spent on phone per day	Most commonly used apps
United States	37	12	3	5 hours	Facebook, Chrome, YouTube
Worldwide	33	12	3	4 hours	Facebook, WhatsApp, YouTube

People Want Fewer Mobile Apps

Today, people use apps to meet their specific needs. For the past few years, app marketplaces featured all kinds of apps for banking, food, medicine, shopping, travel, socializing, dating, delivery service, music, and so on. It's nice to have such a variety of apps, but the number of app downloads per month by smartphone users in the United States as of June 2017 started declining (Figure 2-1), according to a report published by Statista.

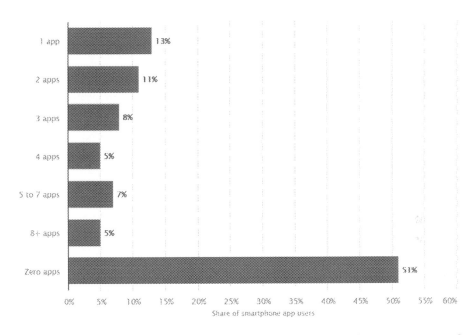

Figure 2-1. *A 51% decline in the downloading of mobile apps per month*

This is not to say that people stopped using apps or that downloads are down overall. We can recognize there are apps for everything and everyone, but people do not need a new app. When we develop a mobile app, we need to think seriously about whether we really need it. Will it help achieve business goals? Will return on investment be high? Most important, will it help customers when needed? In general, customers' expectations are that they want to access information and they want their requests processed faster. Think about ordering food from a restaurant and buying groceries. In this case, you need two different apps that need to be downloaded and accessed individually to place orders. It is a clumsy user experience to have to switch between mobile apps. And if there is a version upgrade, users need to install that. It is most inconvenient to switch constantly among a bunch of applications on your mobile device. Furthermore, whenever you have new requirements, such as buying shoes, for example, you are forced to download the relevant app.

With chatbots, life is simpler. You do not need to download it or reinstall new versions. You simply ask the chatbot to process your request. The same bot provides timely updates on delivery. It is easy to use a chatbot; all you need to do is search for a chatbot in a messaging app and then start chatting. It's all about enhancing the customer experience and developing business growth—and chatbots are an important factor.

Apps Have Become a Tough Business

In today's world, when people want to access information faster than the speed of light, people get tired of downloading new apps, which gives businesses scope for innovation. If we Google "app download statistics," in most cases we'll find statistics that prove app downloads are OK. There are currently 2 million mobile apps available for iOS devices and 2.1 million available for Android devices. Given these numbers, it's understandably difficult for a new app to get noticed. From 2016 to 2017, app growth was 32%. Growth predicted for 2017 to 2021 is 78% over 5 years, with an average increase of just 15%, which is less than many companies would like (Figure 2-2).

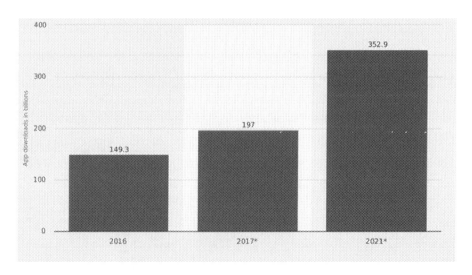

Figure 2-2. *Mobile app download statistics*

We must also keep in mind that mobile apps are not web sites, and it is mandatory to update them. Every year, new OS versions are released, which must be updated; otherwise, the app becomes unsupported on the latest devices and people stop using it. Designs must be updated with the latest trends. Failing to update an app design may degrade the customer experience. Apps survive only when continuous development is planned.

You do not have to compete with apps. Chatbots allow you to set up a business where people already spend most of their time on mobile devices: in a messenger app.

People Use Messengers More Than Other Types of Apps

The easiest way to grow your online business and reach a larger audience is to connect with people where they already spend most of their time. Chatbots help you do this. To get an idea of what people do most on their mobile devices, let's look at Figure 2-3, which shows the most popular apps today, based on the estimated number of downloads published by Statista.

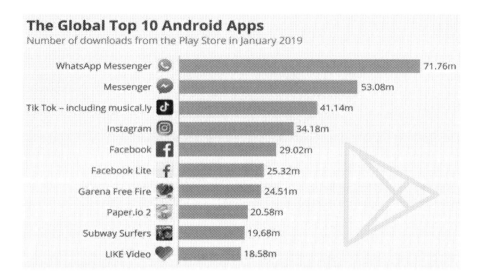

The Global Top 10 Android Apps
Number of downloads from the Play Store in January 2019

App	Downloads
WhatsApp Messenger	71.76m
Messenger	53.08m
Tik Tok – including musical.ly	41.14m
Instagram	34.18m
Facebook	29.02m
Facebook Lite	25.32m
Garena Free Fire	24.51m
Paper.io 2	20.58m
Subway Surfers	19.68m
LIKE Video	18.58m

Figure 2-3. *Popular downloaded apps in 2019*

As we can see in Figure 2-3, people are using messengers more than social networks. Figure 2-4 shows another chart, published by BI Intelligence in 2019, that indicates that messenger apps have only recently overtaken social networking apps in the number of monthly active users.

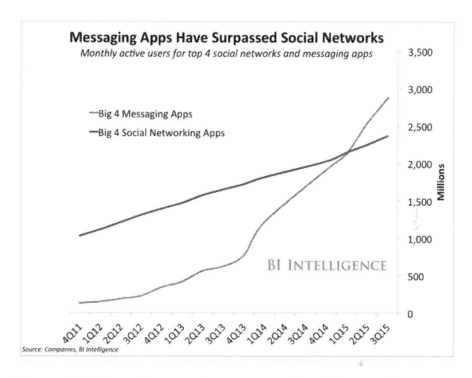

Messaging Apps Have Surpassed Social Networks

Monthly active users for top 4 social networks and messaging apps

Figure 2-4. Messaging apps have surpassed social networks

Chatbots, which live on messenger platforms, have a greater potential to reach large audiences. Therefore, it is possible to provide app services via messenger platforms without any need for a dedicated app. Facebook Messenger, for example, has more than 800 million users, and with a chatbot onboard, you can reach all of them. Times have changed; earlier, people used messaging apps for exchanging texts and graphics, but now these messaging apps have developed into platforms, with APIs for custom development. People now use messaging apps to interact with brands.

Scale Your Business Using Chatbots

By adopting bots, organizations can scale up their business. Imagine you are a mobile device service provider and, through Facebook Messenger, a couple of users connect with you to resolve their queries linked to their mobile devices. Using Facebook Messenger, you can resolve their problems, which is similar in terms of convenience when you chat with friends or family members. If more than 100 users contact you to resolve problems linked to their mobile devices, one employee cannot to manage such a mammoth task in a timely manner. You would need to hire more than 100 employees. But why hire 100 employees when chatbots can do the job and simplify complex business situations? This AI solution allows you to manage your customers efficiently and scale your business.

Realize Cost-effectiveness

For mobile app development specific to your business needs, you definitely need to work with professional iOS and Android developers, and user interface/user experience designers to create a best-in-class product that provides a better customer experience than your competitors. You can use DevOps or Agile methodology to complete development faster. From the project start date until the launch of your app, a lot of time is expended and there are heavy development costs. There may also be delays in a project that also increase costs. Chatbots allow businesses to provide their services efficiently—at a lower cost than an app development project. But even if larger businesses have the money to build a dedicated mobile app, it's still worth considering a more economical solution in the form of a chatbot.

In addition to the app development effort, there are other tasks, such as testing, user acceptance testing, documentation preparation, and quality control, all of which need to be completed before the app is submitted to app stores and before users can access its services. You also need to develop a product road map to enhance your mobile app continuously with new features, a new look-and-feel, and technology upgrades. App maintenance is sometimes very costly and inconvenient, and it requires a constant investment to be successful in the app marketplace.

Everything about chatbots is much simpler. There is no need to worry about app development, because messenger apps are built by third parties. Furthermore, chatbots feature updates that can be done with continuous integration to the back end.

Realize Better Marketing and Increased Sales

The working of chatbots depends on the type of industry. For example, business-to-business (B2B) chatbots help you purchase goods and services; retail chatbots allow you to order groceries; bank chatbots provide you with banking services; food chatbots are used to order food; trading chatbots can deal with your shares; content chatbots can share content that you like; booking chatbots can book hotels, movies, trains, and flights; and the list goes on and on. Chatbots can be useful for any industry. They can help you streamline your business operations, increase efficiency, and improve marketing and sales.

Chatbots can create a personalized experience for your customers by promoting sales or the launch of new products by sending notifications to your customers. Posting such information on your web site or social media accounts, such as on the company Facebook page or in the company's Twitter account, does not help to increase engagement compared to e-mail marketing, for which the same message is sent by e-mail to all your customers.

Benefits of Chatbots

We have now come to the last section in this chapter, where we examine the benefits of chatbots. The 2018 state-of-chatbot report was published based on a survey that had more than 1,000 respondents age 18 to 64 years.

This report was a joint collaboration among Drift, SurveyMonkey, Audience, Salesforce, and myclever. The initial survey question was about online services people use today, such as search engines, product/service web sites, and mobile apps. Respondents were also asked what was the most frustrating about these services.

- Thirty-four percent of respondents said it was hard to navigate web sites.

- Thirty-one percent could not find answers to simple questions such as names and addresses.

- Twenty-eight percent could not find information such as phone numbers.

The online service experience and the user experience are not at the same level, and hence there is a lot of frustration. Figure 2-5 shows predicted use cases for chatbots preferred by users.

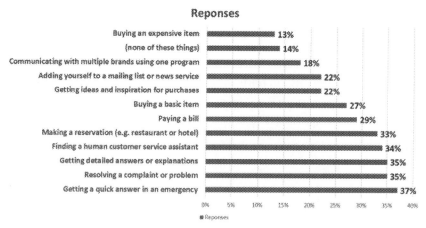

Figure 2-5. *Predicted chatbot use cases*

When you analyze the survey responses to what users would use a chatbot for, 37% of respondents said to find quick answers during an emergency, 35% said to resolve a complaint, and 35% said to get detailed explanations. Interestingly, 34% experienced a human component when interacting with chatbots. Chatbots are the answer to consumer frustration. And if the chatbot cannot help, then consumers want that chatbot to connect them with a human.

Survey respondents gave interesting answers when asked about the benefits they would like to enjoy from using chatbots (Figure 2-6).

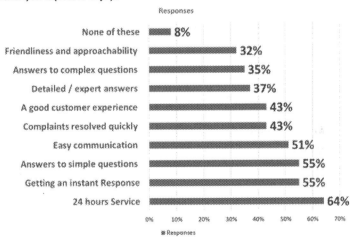

If chatbots were available (and working effectively) for the online services that you use, which of these benefits would you expect to enjoy?

Figure 2-6. *Benefits of using chatbots*

Sixty-four percent of respondents answered that 24-hour connectivity with a chatbot would make them happy. Fifty-five percent said getting answers to questions would be helpful. Chatbots can provide a real-time, on-demand experience to users. Benefits were split between millennials and baby boomers (Figure 2-7).

Millennials versus Baby Boomers

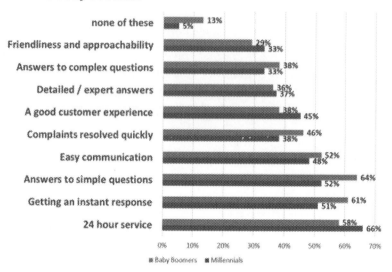

Figure 2-7. *Chatbot benefits: millennials vs. baby boomers*

After comparing responses, the results revealed that 24% of baby boomers need chatbots in their day-to-day life, which shows that chatbots are a requirement for millennials and baby boomers as well. The same survey respondents identified potential drawbacks for using chatbots (Figure 2-8).

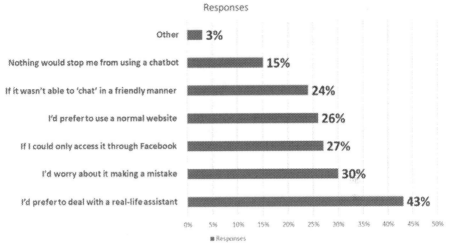

Figure 2-8. *Potential drawbacks for chatbot use*

Responses were contrary to benefits expressed earlier; 43% preferred a human touch, 30% worried about mistakes made by chatbots, and 30% expressed concern about being locked in to using chatbots only through Facebook. However, 15% said nothing would stop them from using chatbots. With this response, it is clear that people would still like to have a human touch in the world of chatbots. Last, respondents were asked to compare the benefits of chatbots vs. mobile apps (Figure 2-9), e-mail (Figure 2-10), and phone (Figure 2-11).

Which of these benefits do you most associate with communicating with businesses?

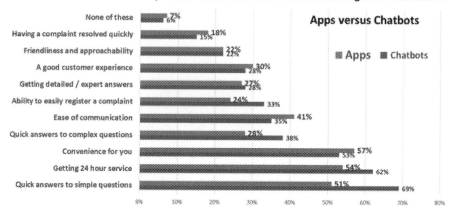

Figure 2-9. *Benefits of chatbots vs. mobile apps*

Which of these benefits do you most associate with communicating with businesses?

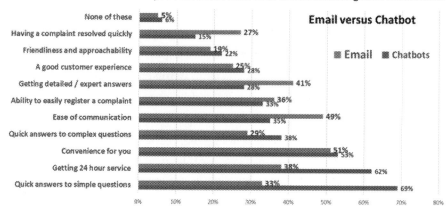

Figure 2-10. *Benefits of chatbots vs. e-mail applications*

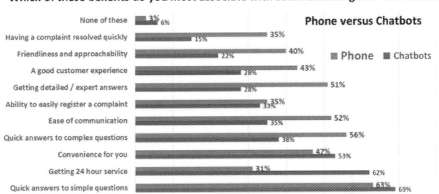

Figure 2-11. *Benefits of chatbots vs. phones*

Consumers preferred chatbots over apps in five of the ten benefit categories, including getting quick answers to simple questions and 24-hour emergency service. When it came to e-mail, consumers preferred chatbots to speedy response times and 24-hour help centers; they provide a definitive edge when it came to getting detailed/expert help. It's a similar story when we compared the benefits of chatbots vs. a phone call. Consumers preferred to use the phone to acquire emergency assistance and to get quick answers to complex questions. E-mail and phone were also considered superior to ease communication and register complaints, getting them resolved in a timely manner.

Summary

In this chapter, we looked at various business scenarios—especially retail businesses—for which the deployment of chatbots results in a better customer experience. We also examined why chatbots are required for business growth, making constructive comparisons between mobile apps and chatbots. Last, we saw the benefits of chatbots as indicated by survey respondents who were millennials and baby boomers.

CHAPTER 3

Design Azure Chatbots

In this chapter, we learn how to design Azure chatbots. We start with an introduction to the Microsoft Bot Framework and examine the start-to-finish workings of chatbots and the requirements necessary for creating Azure chatbots. Last, we look at a real implementation of an Azure chatbot.

Introduction to the Microsoft Bot Framework

In 2016, Microsoft released Bot Framework to develop intelligent applications. This framework was designed to be used for customized development and deployment in channels such as Skype, Facebook Messenger, and Telegram. Bot Framework has many advantages and its services communicate easily with different applications. Skype–Cortana integration (the best example) is used to gather information such as news, weather, tips, and tricks. Using the Microsoft Bot Framework, real-time functionalities, such as booking a hotel and ordering food online, and FAQ readers are developed using communication channels such as Skype, Slack, e-mail, and GroupMe. With the help of bots, it is easy to connect across platforms and go serverless.

© Charles Waghmare 2019
C. Waghmare, *Introducing Azure Bot Service*,
https://doi.org/10.1007/978-1-4842-4888-1_3

To build bot applications using this framework, we can use .NET Software Development Kit (SDK) and Node.js SDK. SDKs help build applications with dialog and built-in prompts to make an interactive application. The REST API is used to develop applications. With such functionality, an application becomes very easy to use and is interactive (Figure 3-1).

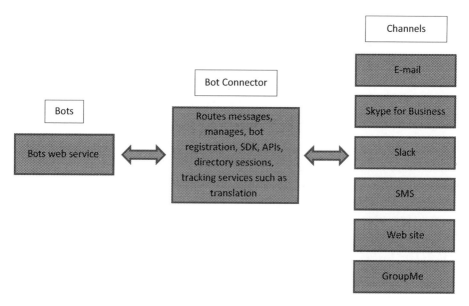

Figure 3-1. *Integration of bots with different online services*

Let's now look at some of the benefits of the Microsoft Bot Framework.

Accelerated Development

Using the Microsoft Bot Framework, you can build, connect, deploy, and manage intelligent chatbots that interact with users through web sites, mobile apps, Cortana, Microsoft Teams, Skype, Slack, Facebook Messenger, and more.

Azure Bot Service provides developers with an integrated environment for chatbot development using Microsoft Bot Framework connectors and bot-builder SDKs. With such functionality, developers can use out-of-the-box templates, such as forms, in business scenarios; and language, questions, and answers can be used for user engagement.

Creation of Intelligent Bots with Cognitive Services

You can build a bot that recognizes users in photos, moderates user content, provides smart recommendations, translates languages, and more. Cognitive Services facilitates your bot in seeing, hearing, understanding, and interpreting in a human way.

User Engagement

Chapter 2 described the integration of chatbots with business applications. Our objective behind the integration of chatbots with other applications is to demonstrate the convenience of an Azure chatbot. A high level of coding is not necessary. Using the standard services available in Azure Portal, integration is easy to achieve.

Cognitive Services: Introduction

Because we are focusing on Azure technology, let's take a look at what Azure Cognitive Services offers. Azure Cognitive Services includes APIs, SDKs, and other services that help developers build intelligent applications without being connected to AI, big data, or background knowledge. Azure Cognitive Services enhances Microsoft machine learning techniques and enables developers to create intelligent applications by adding cognitive features such as emotions, speech and vision recognition, facial interpretation, video detection, and speech and language understanding into their applications. The ultimate goal of Azure Cognitive Services is to help developers build smart applications that can see, speak, hear, understand, interpret, and reason. The following lists the different categories of Azure's vision, speech, language, search, and knowledge APIs.

Vison API

- *Computer vision:* Provides access to process images by the system and returns the correct image or information.

- *Custom vision service:* Builds custom image classifiers.

- *Content moderator:* Helps to monitor and track possible offensive, undesirable content and virus attacks.

- *Face API:* Accesses advanced face algorithms and enables functionalities such as facial detection and recognition.

- *Emotion API:* Accepts an image as an input and provides output (such as anger, fear, shame, surprise, and others) across a set of emotions for each face in the image.

- *Video indexer:* Enables developers to pull insights from video.

Speech APIs

- *Speech service:* Adds speech-enabled features to applications.

- *Custom speech service:* Creates customized language models and acoustic models compatible with your application and users.

- *Bing Speech API:* Searches content using speech.

- *Translator speech:* Performs language translation.

- *Speaker recognition:* Allows identification and verification of speakers based on algorithms.

Language APIs

- *Bing Spell Check:* Performs contextual grammar and spell checking.

- *Language understanding service (LUIS):* Allows your application to understand what a person wants in their own words.

- *Linguistic analysis:* Provides NLP tools to identify text structure.

- *Text analytics:* Provides NLP for raw text to perform sentiment analysis, key phrase extraction, and language detection.

- *Translator text:* Provides machine-based text translation in close to real time.

- *Web language model:* Allows for NLP word prediction, sequencing, completion, and breaking strings of word without spaces.

Search APIs

- *Bing News Search:* Returns a list of news articles relevant to a user's query.

- *Bing Video Search:* Returns a list of videos relevant to a user's query.

- *Bing Web Search:* Returns a list of search results relevant to a user's query.

- *Bing Autosuggest:* Allows you to send a partial search query to Bing and prepopulates suggested queries.

- *Bing Custom Search:* Allows you to create custom search experiences.

- *Bing Entity Search:* Returns information about entities relevant to a user's query.

- *Bing Image Search:* Returns a display of images relevant to a user's query.

- *Bing Visual Search:* Returns insights about images, such as visually similar images and shopping sources for products found in the image.

Knowledge APIs

- *Custom decision service:* Helps to create intelligent systems for contextual decision making, personalizing and optimizing the user experience.

- *QnA Maker:* Allows you to create a question-and-answer service from your semistructured content.

Cognitive services available in Azure support the following languages to allow users to communicate with your applications in a natural way:

- Chinese

- English

- French

- German

- Italian

- Japanese

- Korean

- Portuguese

- Spanish

Different Types of Chatbots Using Azure Bot Service

Azure Bot Service provides different types of bot services that help create and deploy chatbots for specific business scenarios. In this section, we examine the background workings of different chatbots, such as commerce, information, knowledge, enterprise, Cortana, and IoT chatbots.

Commerce Chatbots

Using Azure LUIS and Azure Bot Service, developers can create conversational interfaces for various business purposes, such as ordering pizza, checking account status, and looking for a new movie, which can transform the user experience. For example, pizza restaurants can process requests using text and audio, and use a speaker-enabled audio service for drive-through orders—all of which complement traditional methods of workers accepting requests over the phone and via e-mail. The workflow in Figure 3-2 is as follows:

1. The customer accesses their mobile app.

2. User authentication occurs using the business-to-consumer (B2C) Azure Active Directory.

3. Using the bot, the user requests information.

4. Cognitive Services processes the natural language request.

5. The response is reviewed by the customer, who has the option to refine information.

6. When the user is satisfied, the chatbot pushes the order through for delivery.

7. Azure Application Insights captures personas.

> **Note**   Personas are virtual trends or views of users who have
> accessed AI-enabled services. They are stored temporarily in the
> system. For example, a user from India asks a chatbot to provide a
> list of all United Nations presidents. This view is stored in the system
> as a persona. If some other user asks a similar question related to the
> United Nations, then the chatbot first references personas to find a
> quick answer before querying the database.

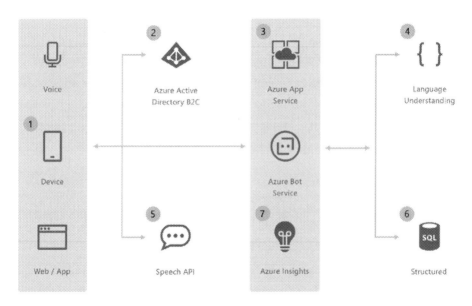

Figure 3-2. *Background workings of commerce chatbots*

Information Chatbots

Informational chatbots are designed to answer questions defined in the
form of a knowledge set or FAQ using Azure Cognitive Services. QnA
Maker attempts to answer more open-ended questions using Azure
Search. A typical workflow is shown in Figure 3-3.

1. A user accesses their device.

2. The Azure Active Directory authenticates the user.

3. The user posts a query inside the chatbot.

4. Cognitive Services returns a FAQ created using QnA Maker.

5. A user defines a valid search string if the FAQ is irrelevant.

6. The chatbot processes the query and submits the query to Azure Search, which returns information based on available data.

7. Application Insights captures the user personas.

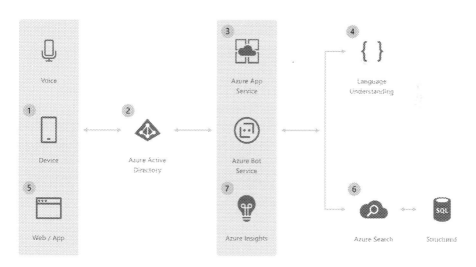

Figure 3-3. *Background workings of information chatbots*

Enterprise Chatbots

Using LUIS and Azure Bot Service, enterprises can build powerful productivity chatbots to streamline common activities by integrating with external systems such as Office 365 Calendar, customer cases stored in Microsoft Dynamics CRM, and much more. A typical workflow is shown in Figure 3-4.

1. A user accesses the enterprise's productivity chatbot.

2. Azure Active Directory authenticates the user's identity.

3. The chatbot queries Office 365 Calendar using Azure Graph.

4. Using data collected from the calendar, the chatbot accesses information in another system (for example, Microsoft Dynamics CRM).

5. Information is returned to the user.

6. Application Insights tracks user personas in the organization.

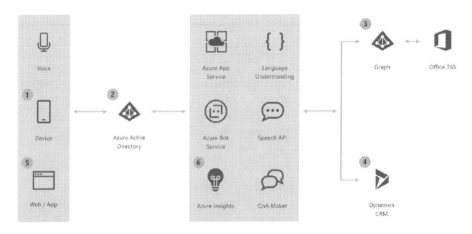

Figure 3-4. *Background workings of enterprise chatbots*

Cortana Chatbot

Using a Cortana chatbot, anybody can schedule a mobile auto maintenance appointment using a cognitive voice service. Cortana chatbots act as a personal assistant. In this example, it helps the user speak with a representative of any auto shop to schedule an appointment. The chatbot can provide users with a list of maintenance services, availability, and time required to implement the service. Before scheduling an appointment, Cortana checks for meeting conflicts and, based on a free slot, an appointment is scheduled. A typical workflow is shown in Figure 3-5.

1. A user access a Cortana chatbot from their device.

2. Using text or voice request, Cortana processes the request.

3. Because of the integration of Cortana with a calendar, conflicts are checked before scheduling an appointment.

4. The chatbot sends a query to the auto service representative regarding available appointment times.

5. The user chooses the appointment time and sends a confirmation.

6. Application Insights analyzes future developments for the Cortana chatbot.

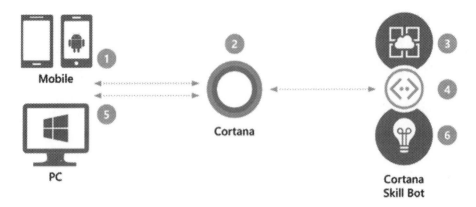

Figure 3-5. *Background workings of a Cortana chatbot*

IoT Chatbots

IoT chatbots make it easy to control devices around the home, such as lighting, using voice or interactive chat commands. A typical workflow is shown in Figure 3-6.

1. A user logs in to Skype and accesses the IoT chatbot.

2. Using voice or text commands, the user requests the IoT chatbot to turn on the lights in their home.

3. The request is transmitted to a third-party service that has access to the IoT device.

4. The request is shared with the user.

5. Application Insights identifies user patterns and generates new ideas for developing IoT chatbots.

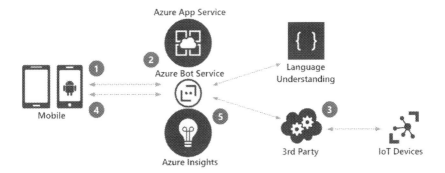

Figure 3-6. *Background workings of IoT chatbots*

IoT chatbots are so simple that users can use channels such as Skype or Slack as chatbots to interact with home devices, as just described.

Designing Chatbots

As we have seen so far in this chapter, the Microsoft Bot Framework allows users to create innovative chatbots to resolve business problems. In the following sections, we look at how to design chatbots that align with best practices and lessons learned.

If you are designing a chatbot, this means you are designing for all people who will be using it. Chatbots can be used over mobile apps, web sites, phone calls, and e-mail, so you need to put in your best effort to make them usable by people over other services they have. The goal of designing a chatbot is to attract users and continue the momentum of its use. To achieve this, it is important to set business goals and identify the precise factors for the chatbot being developed.

Most successful web sites and apps deliver good user experiences, and chatbots are no different in this regard. Therefore, when designing your chatbot to produce a good user experience, priority should be given to the user experience factor. Other factors include the following:

- Chatbots should resolve user problems with a minimal number of steps (in other words, minimal user interactions between the bot and the user).

- Priority should be given to resolve problems better, easier, and faster to produce a good user experience.

- Chatbots should be integrated with frequently used applications or platforms.

- Chatbots should be easy to find.

None of these factors is linked to the intelligence of the chatbot or the cognitive services with which the chatbot is enabled. From a user perspective, as long as the problem is resolved with a minimal number of steps and it delivers a good user experience, users do not care about the technicalities of a chatbot. A great chatbot user experience does not require users to type too much, talk too much, repeat themselves, or explain things the chatbot should know. The process of designing a successful chatbot can be compared with successful web sites or mobile apps that improve through lessons learned and user feedback; the same applies to chatbots.

Some Factors Do Not Guarantee Bot Success

When designing your bot, be aware that none of the following factors necessarily guarantee its success:

- *The intelligence of the bot:* Not all chatbots are designed with cognitive services such as sound, text, image, and others, and many bots have little advanced machine learning or natural language capabilities. A chatbot may include these capabilities if it is designed to resolve business problems. However, there is no link between chatbot intelligence and user adoption of the chatbot.

- *Best vocabulary:* The chatbot you design may have the best vocabulary or the ability to engage users in useful conversation or jokes, but unless it addresses business problems, these capabilities have less importance. Some chatbots have no conversational capability but still produce a great user experience.

- *Cognitive experience:* You need to be careful when considering a cognitive experience with, for example, voice recognition. Sometimes this capability is frustrating for users. Therefore, think of business problems, then think twice about whether voice recognition will resolve those problems. Otherwise, a great user experience is not necessarily one that creates a chatbot that produces "noise," which may disturb users and groups of users.

The First Impression of a Chatbot Really Matters

When we develop a mobile app, the first user interface we think of showing to users is a menu as soon as they open a mobile app. From there, they navigate to different places in the app. Intuitively, looking at the user interface, users understand different areas, such as the About Us page, team details, downloading, privacy policy, and others. When we develop a chatbot, we need to think similarly. Let's look at a couple chatbot user interfaces.

In Figure 3-7, the first user interface starts with an open-ended question: How can I help you? If users do not know what the chatbot can do, there is strong possibility they may get confused and ask a number of queries to resolve issues. If the chatbot doesn't explain what it can do, how will users know its capabilities?

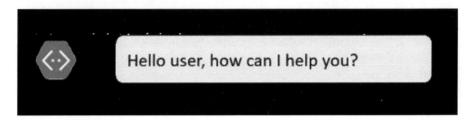

Figure 3-7. *Design 1 of chatbot user interface*

If you look at design 2 in Figure 3-8, it looks very precise. In this user interface, the chatbot definitely informs users of what it can do. If you provide menu options, as in the case of mobile apps, users are likely to find information with a minimal number of steps. In addition, having menus in place saves users time by not requiring them to enter text or too many character the chatbot may not understand. With menu options, users can access information with one click.

Figure 3-8. _Design 2 of chatbot user interface_

Menu options do not necessary imply the chatbot is intelligent; however, they help to provide a better user experience. In addition to a menu, you can also add a form and, based on user input, the chatbot can parse input to relevant information. You can pose more specific questions in the user interface. For example, if your chatbot can effect pizza delivery, it could ask: What type of crust do you want for your pizza? The options could be as follows:

- Thin

- Pan

- Double

On making that selection, another question could pop up: What kind of pizza do you want?

- Vegetarian

- Chicken

- Meat

77

And so on. Posing specific questions takes users to destinations and produces a better user experience. Another important aspect: If your chatbot collects personal data, the chatbot user interface should have a privacy policy and inform users for what purpose and in what manner their data will be used.

Conversation Flow

In general, web sites or mobile apps have multiple user interfaces that are nothing but multiple screens. These user interfaces are connected with each other and, based on input provided in the user interface, redirection to another user interface takes place. Mostly, web sites or mobile apps have one main screen where all navigation links to other user interfaces are present, or users are asked to enter some other input before being redirected to an alternate screen. User interfaces consist of visually appealing designs and colors. To conclude, web sites and mobile apps contain user interfaces that need to be designed meticulously so that users do not get confused while navigating to different links. In addition, they should be able to reach the home page from any other user interface.

Similarly, chatbots also have multiple user interfaces, with one being the main user interface, similar to web sites and mobile apps. But user interfaces in chatbots contain dialog so the user can interact with the chatbot. Dialog can instruct users to take action before they get their results. The chatbot user interface could be plain text, with dialog to links or images, or it could be an input form where users are forced to enter information to get output.

Dialogs help developers to separate various scenarios and build user interfaces for each corresponding scenario. For example, developers can create a different dialog for users to choose their type of pizza crust and another dialog for users to make a payment after order confirmation.

Figure 3-9 shows the flow of a traditional application compared to the dialog flow of a bot.

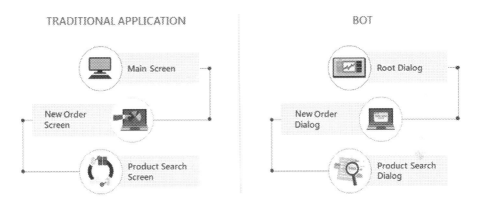

Figure 3-9. *Comparison conversation flow in a traditional application vs. a chatbot*

In Figure 3-9, we see the traditional app's main screen invokes a New Order user interface, which remains in control until it is either closed or invokes another user interface. When the New Order user interface is closed, the user is redirected to the main screen. The user has to navigate multiple user interfaces.

With a chatbot, everything begins with the root dialog. The root dialog invokes the New Order dialog. The New Order dialog is in control until it invokes other dialog or closes it. If the New Order dialog closes, then control of the conversation is returned to the root dialog. The user interface stays the same even if the flow of information is the same as in the web app.

Dialog Stack

A dialog stack is when one dialog invokes another; the chatbot builder adds new dialog to the stack of dialogs. Dialog set at the top of the stack is in control of the conversation with the user. Every new message sent by the user during a conversation is processed by dialog, which is at the top of the stack until it is closed or redirects to another dialog. After the dialog is closed, it is removed from the stack and returns to the previous dialog in the stack, which takes control. Understanding the concept of how a dialog stack is constructed and deconstructed by the chatbot builder is important.

Dialogs, Stacks, and Humans

During the actual working of a chatbot, users navigate across dialogs, create a dialog stack, and return to where they started. Referring back to Figure 3-9, the user starts with the root dialog, invokes the New Order dialog, and, finally, the Product Search dialog. At the final stage, the user selects a product, confirms it in the Product Search dialog, and completes the order. The user exits the New Order dialog after the order is confirmed, then arrives back at the root dialog. In an ideal situation, users follow a linear path, but this doesn't happen often because people frequently change their mind. Let's consider the example in Figure 3-10.

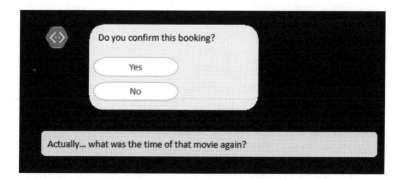

Figure 3-10. *User dialog*

Although the bot may have constructed a logical stack of dialogs, users may decide to do something entirely different or ask a question unrelated to the current topic. In Figure 3-10, the user asks a question instead of providing the yes-or-no response expected. How should the chatbot dialog respond?

- Force the user to answer the first question.

- Attempt to solve the user's question and then move back to yes/no question.

- Disregard all previous dialog, reset the entire dialog stack, and start from the beginning.

There is no right answer to this question. The best solution to this kind of situation is related to the scenario and the way the user expects the chatbot to respond. As conversation becomes complex, managing dialog stacks becomes complex. For complex branching situations, it is easy to create a logical flow to keep track of user conversations.

Design Bot Navigation

We navigate web sites and apps using menus, which are not used when working with chatbots. As seen in the previous sections, users do not necessarily interact with chatbots in linear way, which makes it challenging to design a chatbot that delivers a good user experience. Consider a few of the following issues that may arise in a nonlinear situation that occurs during a user conversation:

- How does the user navigate backward and forward during a conversation?

- How can the user cancel the operation (such as a request for nearby hotels, for example) during a conversation?

- How you can ensure the user does not "get lost" during the conversation?

- How can the user access the main menu (if there is one) during a conversation?

Specifics of bot navigation design depend largely on the features and functionality that your bot supports. To avoid the common pitfalls of poorly designed conversational interfaces, here are five personalities to help you improve your chatbot design:

1. The stubborn chatbot

2. The clueless chatbot

3. The mysterious chatbot

4. The Captain Obvious chatbot

5. The unforgetting chatbot

The Stubborn Chatbot

The stubborn bot insists on maintaining the current course of the conversation, even though the user might steer into a different context. Consider the scenario in Figure 3-11.

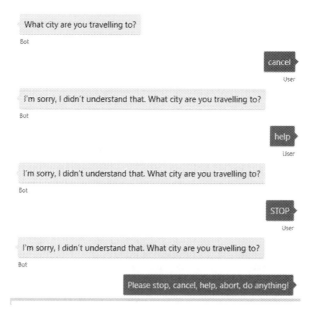

Figure 3-11. *The stubborn chatbot*

To handle this type of situation, know that users can move out of context at any time. If chatbots ask the same question repeatedly when users move out of context, the chatbot is not called a "smart" bot. There is a good chance the user's frustration level will increase and lead to a bad user experience.

The Clueless Chatbot

Clueless chatbots respond in a nonsensical manner when they do not understand user requests. A user may use common words such as *help* or *cancel*, with the expectation that the chatbot will understand and deliver the proper answer. Consider the scenario in Figure 3-12.

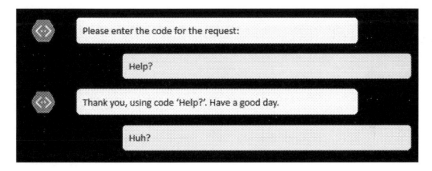

Figure 3-12. *The clueless chatbot*

Ideally, we want to design chatbots to cover all possibilities, but this is close to impossible because we cannot predetermine user behavior. In the scenario presented in Figure 3-12, we can make use of middleware functionality, which logs every message and query in external data sources. By defining the logic in the middleware, we make information accessible to every exchange with the user.

The Mysterious Chatbot

The mysterious chatbot fails to acknowledge the user's input immediately. Consider the scenario in Figure 3-13.

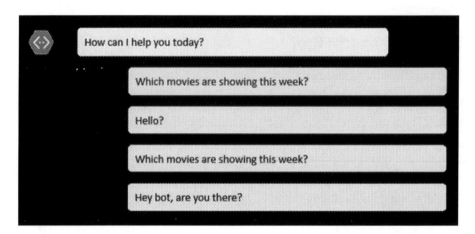

Figure 3-13. *The mysterious chatbot*

The chatbot could be in an outage state or could be compiling the user request. Both situations produce a poor user experience. Therefore, it is important to indicate to the user that the chatbot is processing input. This can be sent in the form of an acknowledgment message or a graphic that indicates user input is being compiled.

The Captain Obvious Chabot

The Captain Obvious chatbot provides unsolicited information that is completely obvious and therefore useless to the user. Consider the scenario in Figure 3-14.

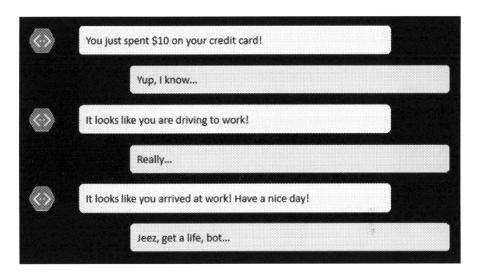

Figure 3-14. *The Captain Obvious chatbot*

Design your chatbot to provide useful information so that users engage and receive a better user experience.

The Unforgetting Chatbot

The unforgetting chatbot integrates information inappropriately from past conversations into the current conversation. Consider the scenario in Figure 3-15.

Figure 3-15. *The unforgetting chatbot*

It is important to maintain the flow of the current conversation to reduce user confusion and frustration, and to increase the chance of users engaging in conversation with the chatbot.

Summary

With this, we come to the end of this chapter. Before moving to the next one, let's look at what we learned. We started with a down-to-earth introduction of the Microsoft Bot Framework and Azure Cognitive Services, looked at the beginning-to-end workings of Azure chatbots, saw different types of Azure chatbots (such as commerce, information, enterprise, and IoT chatbots) and, last, studied chatbot design and design challenges

CHAPTER 4

Design Messages in Chatbots

In this chapter, we focus on how we can create messages effectively in chatbots to build a better customer experience. We aim to develop an understanding of the customer experience, design messages in chatbots with various messaging properties, and see how to create a rich and intuitive customer experience by adding controls and card functionalities in the messages. Let's being with an introduction to customer experience.

Customer Experience: An Introduction

A couple of decades ago, the software business revolved around software development, implementation, and application management services. Then came the era when many innovative mobile devices were launched; apps were developed; analytics such as sentiment analysis, social media command centers, dashboards, and Power BI were launched; and, finally, infrastructures moved into the cloud and we saw Office 365, Amazon Web Services, and software-as-a-service products. Today, we are living in a world of digital transformation in which product companies launch new technologies to create better customer experiences. The realm of digital transformation includes various technologies such as Azure, AI, chatbots, cognitive services, Pega, Liferay, C4Hana, SAP Hybris, salesforce marketing, commerce clouds, Microsoft CRM Dynamics, Jira, and more. IT companies use these technologies to create a digital customer experience.

Currently, there is paradigm shift in which both product and service companies aim to create a great customer experience. What exactly *is* a great customer experience? A customer experience is said to be a combination of the reactions, emotions, and perceptions a customer experiences while using different media to interact or collaborate with a business, product, or employee.

Customer experience builds the bridge between customer and organizational business goals. Success is achieved by creating a connection between the customer experience and customers' needs in such a way that delivers business value at an accelerated pace for the business and the customer.

Figure 4-1. *What is the customer experience?*

In this chapter, we focus on the great customer experience produced by Azure chatbots. However, to produce a great customer experience, we need to design the user experience in the chatbot. Let's look at how to design a chatbot to create a great user experience.

Chatbots for a Greater Customer Experience

Azure chatbots can be designed using various features such as buttons, images, text, and rich cards displayed in the form of a list or carousel. If the chatbot sits inside channels such as Facebook Messenger, Slack, Skype for Business, and others, then rendering these features depends on the channels. There are cases when features are not supported by channels. In these situations, the channel tries to "down-render" the message contents in the form of text or as a static image, which affects appearance. There are exceptional cases when a channel cannot support a few features at all. For example, GroupMe clients installed on devices cannot display a typing indicator while interacting with a user.

Rich User Controls

Rich user controls are common user interface controls such as buttons, images, carousels, and menus that the bot presents to the user and with which the user engages to communicate choice and intent. A bot can use a collection of user interface controls to mimic an app or can even run embedded within an app. When a bot is embedded within an app or web site, it can represent virtually any user interface control by leveraging the capabilities of the app that is hosting it.

Web site developers have been using modern user interfaces to engage users with mobile apps or web sites to produce a great user experience. The same philosophy can be adopted by chatbots by using modern user controls to understand user expectations. When booking an airline ticket, if the chatbot shows a Book Ticket button at the end, then it is convenient for users to achieve expectations with a single action, rather than forcing users to type "book ticket" so the bot can proceed with the booking. The latter case may contain typos, which results in a delay and confusion for the user and the chatbot. As another example, if a user wants to know nearby restaurants and the chatbot can display the top-five nearby restaurants from a Form button, it is quite convenient for the user to make a choice, which creates a good customer experience.

Cards

Cards allows chatbots to display their message in the form of visual, audio, and/or selectable messages, and assist in conversation flow. If a user is required to select an item from a set list, the chatbot can then display a carousel of cards, each containing an image, text for instructions, and one button for making a choice. If a user wants to select multiple items from a given list, then the chatbot can display a smaller single image and a collection of buttons with various options for the user to make a choice. Cards provide in-depth information using audio or video output, or receipts that detail a shopping experience, for example. There are different kinds of cards available and each depends on the business requirement for which the chatbot was developed. Cards create a seamless engagement with users. Let's look at some different kinds of cards, the type of action they promote, and their recommended use.

Microsoft Bot Service cards are objects that can be programmed. They contain standardized collections of rich user controls compatible with a wide range of channels, such as Facebook Messenger, Slack, Skype, and others. The following is a list of cards available with Microsoft Bot Service and the best way to use them effectively in chatbots.

- *Adaptive cards:* Adaptive cards (Figure 4-2) are typically used for cross-channel card deployment. They can adapt the look and feel of the host channel.

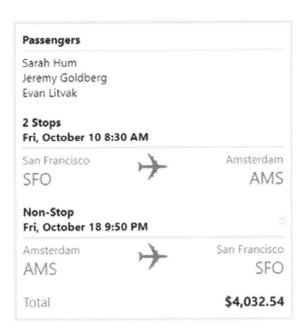

Figure 4-2. *Sample adaptive card*

- *Animation cards:* Animation cards (Figure 4-3) play GIFs or short videos.

Figure 4-3. *Sample animation card*

- *Audio cards:* Audio cards (Figure 4-4) are used to play audio.

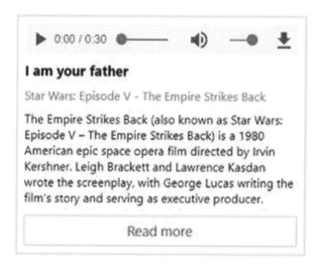

Figure 4-4. *Sample audio card*

- *Hero cards:* Hero cards (Figure 4-5) typically contain a single picture, with text and multiple buttons. They are used to highlight the user's choice visually.

Figure 4-5. *Sample hero card*

- *Thumbnail cards:* Thumbnail cards (Figure 4-6) contain one thumbnail image, text, and multiple buttons. They are used to highlight buttons visually for the user.

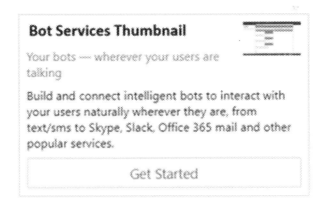

Figure 4-6. *Sample thumbnail card*

- *Receipt cards:* Receipt cards (Figure 4-7) provide comprehensive receipts to users that list the items purchased by the user.

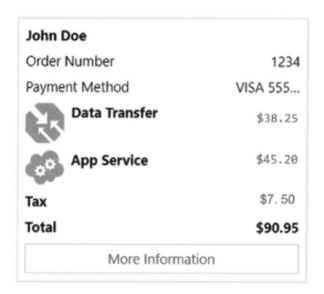

Figure 4-7. *Sample receipt card*

- *Sign-in cards:* Sign-in cards (Figure 4-8) are used to enable user login. These cards normally contain text with instructions and one or more buttons for users to make a choice.

Bot Services Sign-in Card

Sign-in

Figure 4-8. *Sample sign-in card*

- *Suggested action cards:* Suggested action cards (Figure 4-9) contain multiple buttons linked to actions. When a button is pushed, the card disappears.

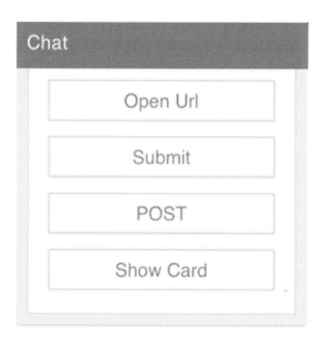

Figure 4-9. *Sample suggested action card*

- *Video cards:* Video cards (Figure 4-10) play videos using a URL or they stream videos.

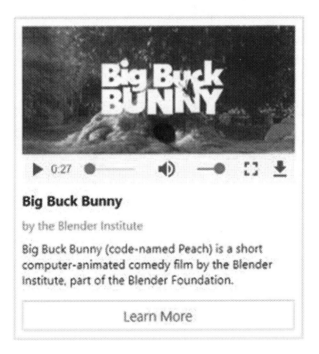

Figure 4-10. *Sample video card*

- *Carousel cards:* Carousel cards (Figure 4-11) are
  presented as a collection that allows users to view, at a
  glance, a series of possible user choices.

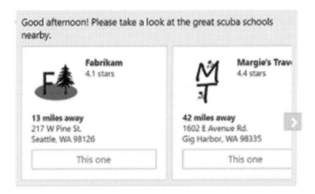

Figure 4-11. *Sample carousel cards*

Cards allow you to design your bot once and have it work across a variety of channels. However, not all card types are fully supported across all available channels.

As stated earlier, an important thing to remember during the design of a chatbot is to use common user interface elements. The principal design objective is to resolve user problems in the most efficient way possible and avoid integration of natural language into the chatbot to make it more complex. Try using the least user interface controls to enable the chatbot to resolve user problems; add other elements if user interface controls cannot help.

Text and Natural Language Understanding

A chatbot accepts input from users in the form of text and has a parsing ability using regular expression matching or natural language understanding APIs such as LUIS. Depending on the type of input provided by the user, natural language understanding may or may not be a good solution. For example, let's say you want your chatbot to request the user's name. For our example, let's assume the user is named Chris. Here are some different possibilities of how Chris will enter his name:

- Chris

- My name is Chris

- Chris Stevens

- Mr. Kris Stevens

A specific question was asked, but the answers may be entered in a variety of formats that may confuse the chatbot, and thus the user, and may lead to a bad user experience. Another open-ended question is: How are you feeling today? Again, a different combination of answers can be expected from users. What is the weather outside? This question can trigger multiple combinations of answers.

The important thing to keep in mind is to ask specific questions without having to use a LUIS service; this helps reduce chatbot complexity. A question such as "How are you feeling?" could have the answers Good, OK, or Bad, allowing the user to make an easy choice. There are DevOps chatbots that run on specific commands used to manage VMs. The Start/VM1 command triggers the first VM to start. The command Reboot/VM2 reboots trigger VM2.

In short, avoid using natural language understanding and ask specific questions, making use of cards and user controls to create a great customer experience and reduce complexity.

Knowledge-based chatbots or question-and-answer chatbots can answer user questions based on documents or information loaded in a database. QnA Maker and Azure Search are both technologies designed specifically for this type of scenario. A user may ask a general question. When designing a chatbot that answers questions based on structured or unstructured data from databases, web pages, or pools of documents, consider using technologies designed specifically to address this scenario. Do not attempt to resolve the problem with natural language understanding such as LUIS.

In a scenario in which users want to order a hamburger, they can engage with a chatbot with questions such as: Where is the nearest burger joint? Where is the nearest MacDonald's within three miles? Show me combo burger offers. In this type of scenario, natural language understanding may be useful, and a LUIS API can extract the main component of words from a user's question to understand intent and provide the desired answer. When developing chatbots using natural language models, it is dangerous to assume that users will provide all the information needed in their questions. However, design your chatbot in such a way that users do not have to repeat the same question in different ways. Request precise information from the user.

There are chatbots that use cognitive technology, such as speech, for input and output. With these chatbots, speech is the only means of communicating with users.

Choosing among Rich User Controls, Text and Natural Language, and Speech

Naturally, human beings like to communicate with each other using a combination of gestures, voice, and symbols. Similarly, one can design chatbots using rich user controls, text, and speech. These communication methods can be joined together; there is no need to choose one over the other. I illustrate this with a cooking example. This particular cooking chatbot shows users recipes in the form of images or videos. To choose a specific recipe, users simply touch the screen (this chatbot is enabled with rich user controls). In addition, users can input information to search for a specific recipe. While designing, incorporate user experience elements that support different ways in which users can interact with a chatbot.

Key Chatbot Message Concepts

At this point, we have learned about the following elements of chatbots: rich user control cards, natural language understanding, and speech techniques that are used while designing chatbots. Now we'll focus on creating messages in chatbots and adding media attachments, rich cards, speech messages, and input/suggested messages. However, before delving into these subjects, let's go through some key concepts used frequently in chatbot development.

Connector

The Bot Frame Connector provides a single REST API that facilitates communication between chatbot and user by transmitting messages from the chatbot using channels such as Skype, e-mail, and Facebook Messenger, and then transmits back from the channels to the chatbot.

Activity

The connector uses an activity object to transmit information back and forth between chatbots and users (i.e., channels). The most common object is message activity, but there are other activity objects:

- *ConversationUpdate:* The chatbot was added to the conversation and users are added or removed from the conversation.

- *ContactRelationUpdate:* The chatbot was added or removed from the user's contact list.

- *Typing:* During a conversation, the user or chatbot is compiling a response.

- *UserDeleteData:* The user has requested the bot to delete user data it may have stored.

- *EndOfConversation:* Marks the end of a conversation

- *Event:* A communication was sent to the user by the chatbot that is invisible or not seen by the user during the chat.

- *Invoke:* The user is requesting the bot to perform a specific operation.

- *MessageReaction:* A user is reacting to the message by, for example, clicking the Like button.

Dialog

Dialog is used to model and manage conversations between a chatbot and users. A dialog maintains a stack of dialogs that are active during a conversation. Dialogs are portable across computers, which makes it possible to scale chatbot implementation.

FormFlow

FormFlow is used to collect information from users during conversations with a chatbot. For instance, when a user wants to order a pizza, the chatbot must get information from the user, such as type of crust, type of pizza, toppings, and so on. With basic guidelines, FormFlow can generate dialogs automatically to manage a pizza order conversation, for example.

State

The Bot Builder Framework has the capability of storing and retrieving state information pertaining to the user, the conversation, and user-specific information within the context of a specific conversation. During a conversation, information present in the state can be reused. In short, the state is a kind of database; in the Bot Builder Framework, data storage is possible in SQL Server.

Now let's focus on message properties that can be used during conversations between users and a chatbot.

Create Messages

During communication with users, chatbots send information to users and receive information from users as well. The information exchange exists in the form of plain text, text to be spoken, suggested actions, media attachments, rich cards, and channel-specific data.

Send a Customized Message

Using the `Activity` object and setting the necessary properties, a custom plain-text message can be shared a with user. The property can be set to plain, markdown, or XML; the default in Bot Framework is markdown. Here is an example:

```
Message - "Hello World"
Message format set - Plain text
```

Attachments

The `Attachments` property of a message activity is used to send and receive media attachments such as images, audio, videos, files, and rich cards.

Entities

The `Entities` property of a message consists of an array of open-ended `schema.org` objects that allow for an exchange of common contextual metadata between the channel and the bot—for example, "mention" someone during a conversation, share location-related information using geographic coordinates or a postal address.

Channel Data

Channel data are used to implement channel-specific functionality, such as creating a custom e-mail message, a full-fidelity Slack message, a Facebook notification, a Telegram message, and a line message.

Text-to-Speak

The Speak property of a message can be used to specify the text to be spoken by a bot on a speech-enabled channel.

Suggested Actions

The SuggestedActions property of a message activity can be used to show buttons that the user can use to submit input. The buttons disappear after the user makes a selection.

Add Media Attachments to Messages

An exchange of messages between a user and a chatbot may contain media attachments (e.g., image, video, audio, file). The Attachments property of the Activity object contains a list of Attachment objects that contain media attachments and rich cards used in the message. The connector service transmits data in such a way that channels are able to retain messages. If the attachment is a file, the hyperlink is displayed in the conversation.

To add a media attachment to a message, create an Attachment object for the message activity and define the ContentType, ContentURL, and Name properties. Here is some sample code in C#:

Listing 4-1. Adding a media attachment

```
replyMessage.Attachments.Add(new Attachment()
{ ContentUrl = "https://www.charleswaghmare.com.png",
    ContentType = "image/png",
    Name = "Charles_waghmare.png"
});
```

Add Rich Card Attachments to Messages

An exchange of a message between a user and a chatbot can contain rich cards in the form of lists or carousels. The Attachments property of the Activity object contains a list of Attachment objects: rich cards and media attachments within the message. Earlier in the chapter, we saw different types of rich cards, such as adaptive, animation, audio, hero, thumbnail, receipt, sign-in, and video.

103

To display rich cards in a list format, set the activity's
AttachmentLayout property to "list"; to display multiple rich cards
in a carousel format, set the activity's AttachmentLayout property to
"carousel". If the carousel format is not supported, then rich cards are
displayed in the list format. Normally, all chatbot responses are created
with adaptive cards. Check out the example in Figure 4-12.

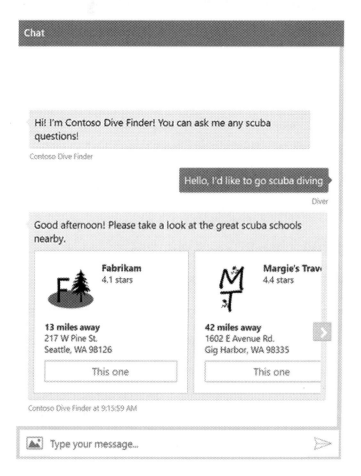

Figure 4-12. *Response using an adaptive card*

Process Events within Rich Cards

To process events within rich cards, there are `CardAction` objects to specify the action that should take place when a user clicks a buttons or taps a card. Here is a list of `CardAction` options:

- *Open URL:* Try opening the URL in the browser.

- *IM Back:* The chatbot receives the text the of message when the user clicks a button or taps a rich card. This message is visible to all participants in the chatbot.

- *Post Back:* The chatbot receives the text of the message when the user clicks a button or taps a rich card. Some channels may display this text in the message feed and it will be visible to all conversation participants.

- *Call:* Then, *Call Destination* with phone call: Tel: 999222

- *Play Audio:* Using this URL of the audio to be played

- *Play Video:* Using this URL of the video to be played

- *Show Image:* Using this URL of the image to be displayed

- *Download File:* Using this URL of the file to be downloaded

- *Sign In:* Using this URL of OAuth flow to be initiated

These card actions are used to add different rich cards to the conversation between the chatbot and the user.

Add Speech to Messages

To create a speech-enabled chatbot, you can construct messages—in other words, precise text to be spoken by the chatbot. You can also influence the state of the user's microphone by specifying an input to indicate whether the chatbot is able to accept, is expecting, or is ignoring the user message. There are multiple ways to specify text to be spoken by a chatbot on a speech-enabled channel. You can use message properties such as Speak, call the IDialogContext.SayAsync() method, and specify prompt options—Speak and retry—in the message prompt.

To specify text to be spoken by a chatbot, you can use a plain-text string or a string that is formatted in Speech Synthesis Markup Language, which is an XML-based markup language that enables you to control various characteristics of your chatbot, such as voice, rate, volume, pronunciation, pitch, and more.

To influence the user's microphone to indicate whether the speech-enabled chatbot is accepting, expecting, or ignoring inputs given by user, the message properties should be set to InputHints.AcceptingInput to indicate the chatbot is ready for input and is not waiting for a response from the user. The Message property should be set to InputHints. ExpectingInput indicates the chatbot is waiting for a response from the user. Last, the Message property should be set to InputHints. IgnorningInput indicates the chatbot is unready to accept input from the user.

Add Suggested Actions to Messages

By adding suggested actions to your conversations, you can tap a button to provide input to a chatbot. Also, users do not have to type text and, as a result, there is an improved user experience that is facilitated by providing intuitive buttons for users to answer questions and select responses from multiple choices. In addition, buttons in the form of cards double the user experience because, as soon as they are tapped, they disappear from the screen. As a result, users are prevented from tapping stale buttons during a conversation.

To add suggested actions to a message, set the `SuggestedActions` property of the activity to a list of `CardAction` objects that represent the buttons to be displayed to the user during a conversation.

Send and Receive Activities

The Microsoft Bot Framework has a REST API that facilitates chatbot and user communication through multiple channels such as Skype, Slack, e-mail, and others. Communication between a chatbot and the user takes place by transmitting a message from the chatbot to the user and vice versa. To create a reply, the connector should use the message activity object to transmit information between the user and the chatbot. Every activity contains information, such as who created the message, the context of the message, and the recipient of the message. By calling Connect with Message activity "Reply to Activity," you can create and send a reply message. Furthermore, you can send a nonreplyable message by calling the message property `SendtoConversation`. The `CreateMessage` activity method helps to create the new message and sets all property values as needed.

To start a new conversation by a chatbot with one or more users, the message activity Create Direct Conversation is used to create a private conversation. The message activity Create Conversation helps to create new conversations and opens them with one or more users. Last, the Send to Conversation method helps in sending newly created messages.

Implement Global Message Handlers

Users commonly attempt to access certain functionalities they have used while interacting with web sites or mobile apps. These common functionalities are help, cancel, or start over. These actions are often used in the middle of a conversation when the chatbot is expecting a different input from the user. By deploying global handlers such as help, cancel, or start over, you can design your chatbot to handle such requests and act accordingly. Check out the example in Figure 4-13.

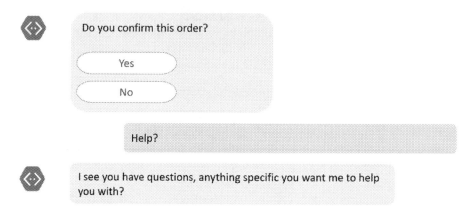

Figure 4-13. *Message handlers*

Intercept Messages

Messages between chatbots and a group of users can be intercepted by middleware functionality in the Microsoft Bot Framework. For each intercepted message, you can save or inspect the message, or create a conversation log. By default, the Bot Framework does not save this information automatically for privacy reasons. It is a best practice to tell users that their conversation with the chatbot is being saved and to explain the specific reason for saving it.

Send Proactive Messages

A chatbot usually sends messages to users that are related directly to the user's prior input. But, in some cases, it is useful for a message not to be related directly to the last message sent by the user. These messages are called *proactive messages*. There are various business scenarios in which proactive messages are useful. If the user has set up a reminder in a bot, then the chatbot will send the reminder in the form of a proactive message when the time for the event is near. Furthermore, a chatbot can be asked to keep a close eye on sales offers and then trigger notifications when there is a dip in price. When this is set up and a price decrease occurs, the chatbot delivers an e-mail notification to the user. In another situation, a user may want to make a hotel reservation based on a price cap. When the chatbot finds a reservation that meets the user's requirement, it sends a notification to the user. Proactive messages are also used to inform users that their input is getting processed or the chatbot is waiting for user input to continue the conversation.

A point to remember before sending proactive messages is not to send multiple proactive messages in a short span of time because this may confuse the user. Also, do not send proactive messages to someone who has never used a bot, because it may result in an unexpected scenario (Figure 4-14).

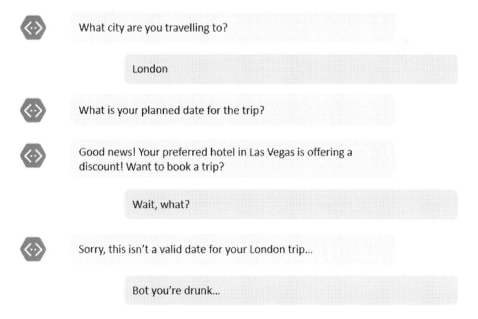

Figure 4-14. *Unexpected proactive message*

In the example in Figure 4-14, we can infer that the user has set up a reminder for hotel prices to drop by certain limit. However, while booking a reservation for a different trip, a notification pops up and the user gets confused. This situation can be handled in a better way, such as displaying reminder setups in a different color, sending notifications after a booking is completed, canceling the current booking and delivering a notification, or interrupting the current booking until the user responds, then switching back to the current booking.

Ad hoc private messages are the simplest form of proactive messages, and chatbots inject them into messages whenever triggered, regardless of whether a user is engaged in a separate conversation with a chatbot. Chatbots can also send a dialog-based proactive message to a user. In this case, the chatbot must first collect and save information from the current conversation.

Summary

With this, we come to the end of this chapter. During our journey in this chapter, we enhanced our familiarity with the customer experience and then examined how we can make conversations between chatbots and users intuitively strong by using rich controls and cards. Last, we looked at connectors and different message properties to help us build conversations in the most efficient and intuitive ways.

CHAPTER 5

Chatbot Integration

In previous chapters, we learned to develop a chatbot from the Azure Portal, connecting it with question-and-answer services, LUIS, and others; developed message templates to engage users; explored different business scenarios in which we can deploy chatbots; and created a better user experience using chatbots. In this chapter, we focus on integrating Azure chatbots with different channels. Again, the approach is simple and clear for both technical and nontechnical readers to understand. The objective of showing the integration of a chatbot with other applications is to demonstrate the convenience behind Azure chatbots in which a high level of coding is not mandatory. By using the standard services available in Azure Portal, integration is easy to achieve.

To start, let's look at integrating Azure with different communication apps. At the end of the chapter, I compare different cloud platforms and show that the Azure platform is the best for chatbot development.

Integration of a Chatbot with Communication Apps

As seen in Figure 5-1, channels such as Facebook Messenger, Kik, WhatsApp, and others can be connected to chatbot. The Microsoft Bot Service, available in Azure Portal, helps to connect chatbots with various channels. The Microsoft Bot Service also helps to facilitate interaction

© Charles Waghmare 2019
C. Waghmare, *Introducing Azure Bot Service*,
https://doi.org/10.1007/978-1-4842-4888-1_5

between chatbots and users. In addition to standard channels such as Facebook Messenger (Figure 5-1), this service also helps connect to nonstandard channels, such as your client's application. For channels, you must provide channel information to run chatbots on that channel. Most channels require your chatbot to have its account on the channel; other channels such as Facebook Messenger demand that your chatbot be registered with the channel as well.

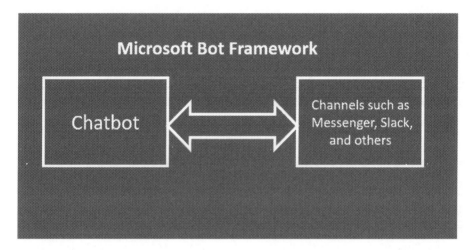

Figure 5-1. *Connection between a chatbot and a communication app*

The Microsoft Bot Framework normalizes messages from the chatbot to the channels. Normalizing procedures involves converting messages from the channel schema to the chatbot schema and vice versa. Let's say you have a situation in which an e-mail greeting is sent from the chatbot schema to the channel schema that cannot be displayed as is because of missing functionalities in the chatbot. In this case, a greeting card is displayed and a link for user action is shown in the channels. Any Azure chatbot you have created (see Chapter 1) can be connected to channels by means of a simple configuration done inside the channels. The configuration to connect the chatbot and the channels is done using the following steps and is shown in Figure 5-2.

1. Sign in to Azure Portal.

2. Choose the chatbot to be configured

3. Under Bot Management, click Channels and choose
   the channel you wish to use.

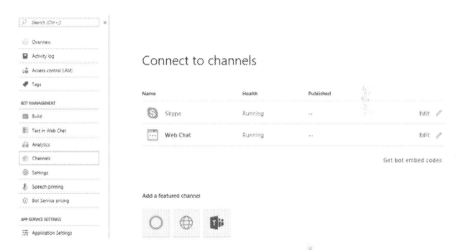

Figure 5-2. *Connecting a chatbot to a channel*

After you post the channel configuration, users can start using the
chatbot on that channel.

Let's now look at connecting chatbots with other channels.

Connect a Chatbot to Cortana

Cortana is a speech-enabled channel that has the capability to receive and
send voice messages along with text. For any chatbot to be connected with
Cortana, it should be designed to accept and receive speech instructions.
Cortana Skill is the name of the chatbot that involves a Cortana client;

publishing any chatbot that connects to Cortana adds the chatbot to Cortana Skill. To integrate with Cortana, as seen in Figure 5-3, follow these steps:

1. Open Azure Portal, then click the Cortana icon in the Channels section.

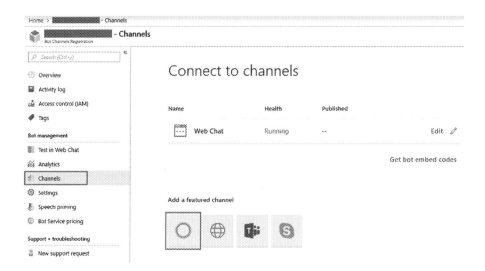

Figure 5-3. *Connecting a chatbot to Cortana*

2. When connecting a chatbot to Cortana, information is required to be updated; this is done in the registration window. Registration consists of the following:

    - *Skill icon:* The icon is displayed in the Cortana canvas when Cortana Skill is involved.

    - *Display name:* The display name is the name of the Cortana Skill chatbot to be displayed in the user interface. It accepts no more than 30 characters.

- *Invocation name:* The invocation name is the name used by users to invoke or call the Cortana Skill chatbot with voice or text. Invocation is part of the essential natural language and is a call, request, or petition to a chatbot to perform an action based on an utterance. An utterance containing more than three words is difficult to recognize or distinguish. "One-way ticket" is easy compared to "two-way train ticket." While invoking, avoid using duplicate names for your chatbot, terms such as *bot* or *chatbot*, homophones such as *wait* or *weight*, hard-to-pronounce words, and names that combine multiple words into one, such as *five-star hotel*.

Users invoke skills by saying the invocation phrases:

Example Invocation Phrases with Connecting Words

- Ask <Invocation Name> to <Utterance>.

- Search <Invocation Name> for <Utterance>.

- Get <Invocation Name> to <Utterance>.

Example Invocation Phrases without User Utterances

- Tell <Invocation Name>

- Start <Invocation Name>

- Run <Invocation Name>

Example Invocation Phrases without Connecting Words

- Ask <Invocation Name> <Utterance>

- Use <Invocation Name> <Utterance>

- Search <Invocation Name> <Utterance>

3. As seen in Figure 5-4, to manage user identity, slide the option to enable it.

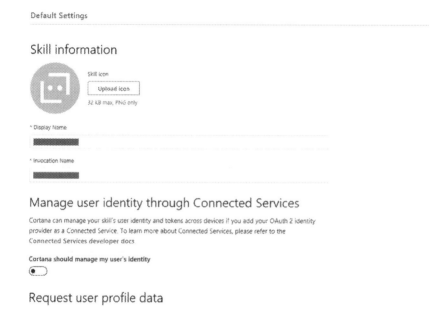

Figure 5-4. *Managing user identity*

As seen in Figure 5-4, upon enabling the option, mandatory and nonmandatory fields need to be updated. In addition, a chatbot must be published in Azure before connecting it to Cortana. To enable user identity, you need to set up the identity (Figure 5-5).

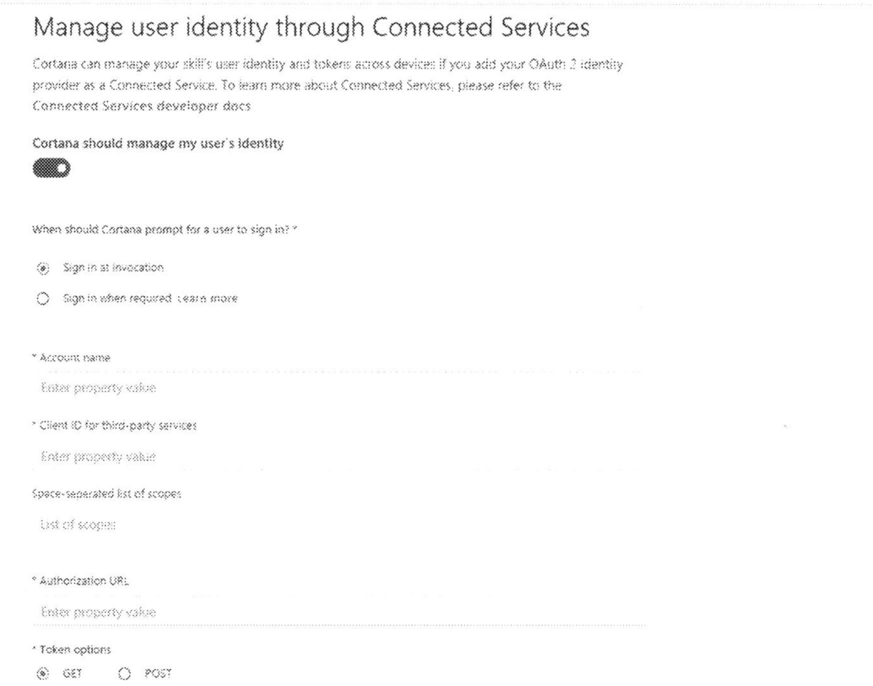

Manage user identity through Connected Services

Cortana can manage your skill's user identity and tokens across devices if you add your OAuth 2 identity provider as a Connected Service. To learn more about Connected Services, please refer to the Connected Services developer docs

Cortana should manage my user's identity

When should Cortana prompt for a user to sign in? ˅

○ Sign in at invocation

○ Sign in when required Learn more

＊ Account name

Enter property value

＊ Client ID for third-party services

Enter property value

Space-separated list of scopes

List of scopes

＊ Authorization URL

Enter property value

＊ Token options

◉ GET   ○ POST

Figure 5-5. *Managing general chatbot information*

- Select "Sign-in at invocation" when you expect Cortana to sign in users when they invoke Skill.

- Select "Sign-in when required" when you do not expect users to sign in with Skill when invoked; rather, they sign in using features such as card attachments.

- Enter the account name, which is the name of the Skill chatbot you would like to be displayed after sign-in.

- Enter the client ID for third-party services. This is your chatbot's application ID and you get it when you've registered your bot.

117

- Enter the space-separated list of scopes. The Scope parameter is a space-separated list of OAuth scopes that indicates which parts of the user's account your app can access. Examples include files, chats, reactions, and searches, followed by classes of actions such as read, write, and history (includes access to direct messages).

- Enter the authorization URL. Set it to `https://login.microsoftonline.com/common/oauth2/v2.0/authorize`.

- Under "Token options," select POST to post the token in the token URL field or select GET to get the token.

- Enter the grant type. To use the code grant flow, use Authorization code or, to use implicit grant flow, select implicit. OAuth gives users limited access to applications. Code grant flow and implicit grant flow are OAuth2.0 specifications for client applications to get an access token that represents user permission for the client application to access their data. These standards are used from a security standpoint.

  - *Authorization code grant:* The user logs in from the client app and the authorization server returns an authorization code to the app. The app then exchanges the authorization code for the access token. It is possible to obtain a prolonged access token; it can be renewed with a refresh token.

  - *Implicit code grant:* The user logs in from the client app and the authorization server issues an access token to the client app directly. This grant type does not allow the issuance of a refresh token.

Here is what to fill in. Refer Figure 5-6 for details:

- Set token URL to `https://login.microsoftonline.com/common/oauth2/v2.0/token`.

- Select HTTP Basic under "Client authorization scheme".

- Do not check the option for Internet access required to authenticate users.

- Select "Request user profile data" (optional), if you want the Skill chatbot to access information such as name, location, workplace, and more. This generates customized messages such as "<Name>, how was your day at <workplace>?"

- Finally, select Deploy Cortana. This brings you to the Channel blade or menu screen. From there, you should see Cortana connected to your chatbot.

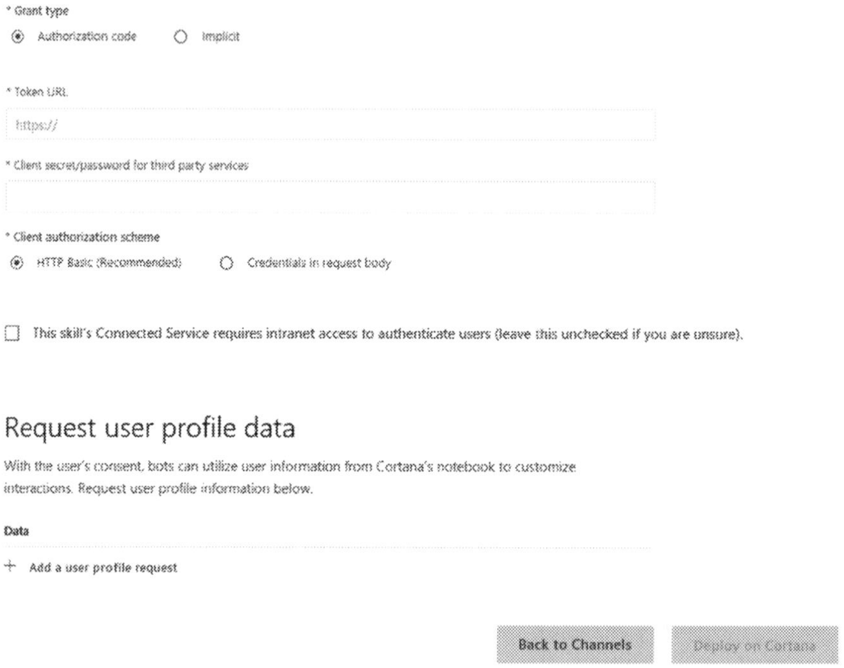

* Grant type

⦿ Authorization code   ○ Implicit

* Token URL

```
https://
```

* Client secret/password for third party services

* Client authorization scheme

⦿ HTTP Basic (Recommended)   ○ Credentials in request body

☐ This skill's Connected Service requires intranet access to authenticate users (leave this unchecked if you are unsure).

Request user profile data

With the user's consent, bots can utilize user information from Cortana's notebook to customize interactions. Request user profile information below.

Data

+ Add a user profile request

Back to Channels   Deploy on Cortana

Figure 5-6. *General Chatbot Information*

Connect a Chatbot to Skype

Skype has been adopted by many organizations for their employees to enable instant messaging and audio and video calls, and to share content. By connecting a chatbot with Skype, users can actually interact with the chatbot in Skype through the Skype interface. To do this, follow these steps:

1. Open Azure Portal, click the Channel blade, and click the Skype icon (Figure 5-7).

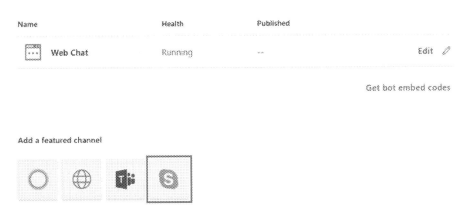

Figure 5-7. Connecting chatbot and Skype

2. After you choose Skype, you need to configure settings for Web control, Messaging, Calling, Groups, and Publish (Figure 5-8).

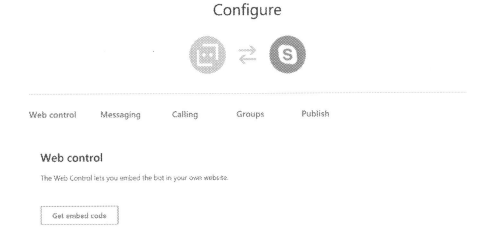

Figure 5-8. Configuring settings for Skype

- *Web control:* Click "Get embed code" to get the embedded code. This code is hosted on your web site or mobile app, at which point the user can interact with the chatbot with Skype in the background. After you click this button, you are redirected back to the Configure screen (Figure 5-8).

- *Messaging:* In Messaging, you configure the manner in which your chatbot sends and receives messages in Skype.

- *Calling:* In Calling, you configure the calling feature of Skype in the chatbot. You can enable it or keep it disabled. If you enable it, use interactive voice response functionality or real-time media functionality.

- *Groups:* In Groups, you configure how to add chatbots to a group for instant group messaging and group calls.

- *Publish:* In Publish, you publish your chatbot enabled with Skype.

Connect a Chatbot to Telegram Messenger

Let's configure a chatbot to communicate with people as Skype using the Telegram Messenger app:

1. To create a new Telegram chatbot, visit BotFather: `https://telegram.me/botfather` (Figure 5-9).

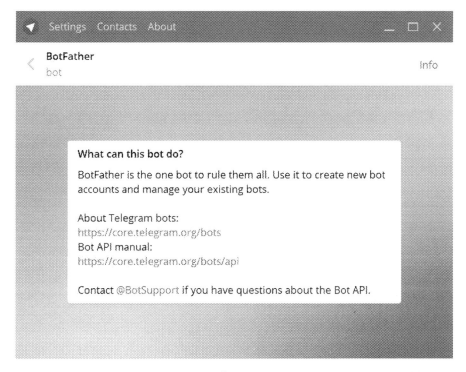

Figure 5-9. *Visiting BotFather*

2. Create a new chatbot using the command /newbot
    to create a new bot (Figure 5-10).

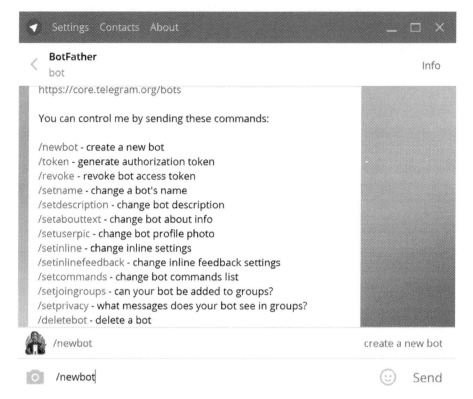

Figure 5-10. Choose the /newbot command to create a new chatbot

3. Assign a friendly name to your Telegram chatbot.
    As you can see in Figure 5-11, we will call our bot
    Delightful Bot.

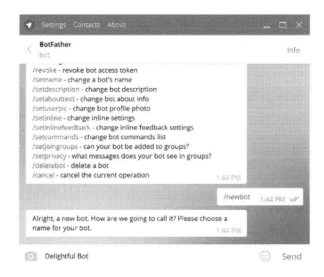

Figure 5-11.   *Give your bot a friendly name*

4.   Specify the username. As you can see in Figure 5-12,
     our username is DelightfulBot.

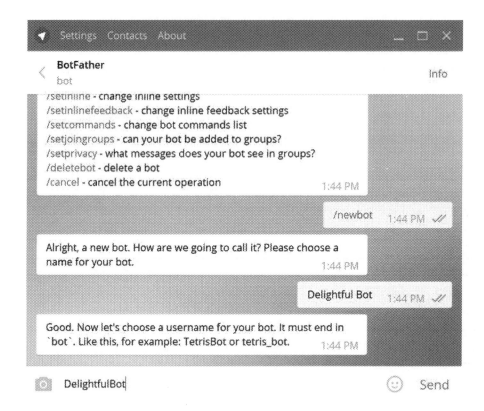

Figure 5-12. *Specify the username*

5. Copy the access token of the Telegram chatbot
(Figure 5-13).

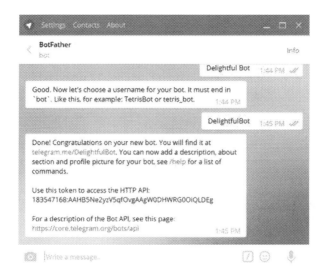

Figure 5-13. *Copy the Telegram chatbot token*

6. Last, open Azure Portal, click the Channel blade,
    click the Telegram icon and paste the access token.
    Then, click Submit and check Enabled. Our chatbot
    is now ready to communicate with Telegram users.

Connect a Chatbot to Kik

Now we'll configure a chatbot to connect to the Kik messaging app to
engage users. Follow these steps:

1. Install the Kik messaging app and sign in using a
    user ID and password (Figure 5-14).

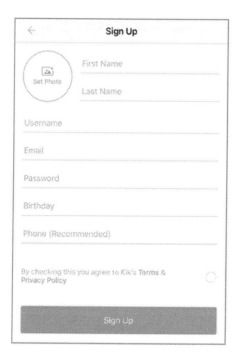

Figure 5-14. *Install the Kik messaging app*

2. After installing the app, log in to the Kik portal using a mobile phone. Then, open the Kik developer's portal (Figure 5-15).

Figure 5-15. *Log in to the Kik developer's portal*

3. Follow the chatbot setup process and give a name to it (Figure 5-16).

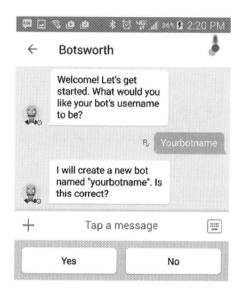

Figure 5-16. *The chatbot setup process*

4. Copy the name and API key from the Configuration tab. Click Save (Figure 5-17).

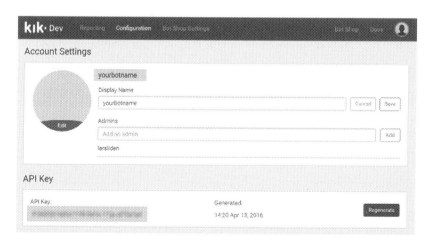

Figure 5-17. *Configuration setup*

5. Open Azure Portal, click the Channel blade, and click the Kik icon. Paste the Kik credentials and enable the chatbot by clicking Submit Kik Credentials.

Bot Name	
API Key	

Submit Kik Credentials

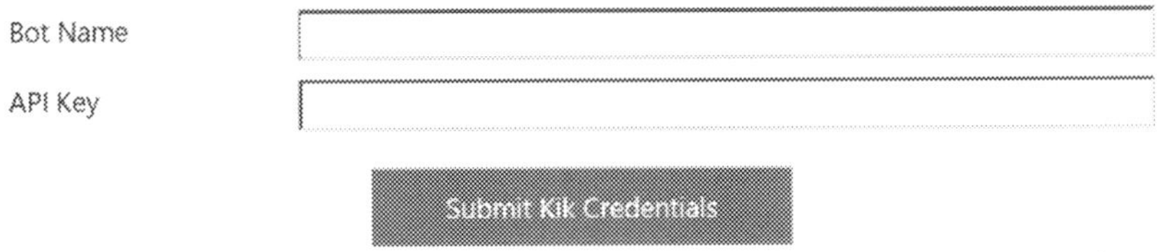

Figure 5-18. *Submit credentials*

Connect a Chatbot to a Direct Line

To connect a chatbot to a direct line, do the following:

1. Open Azure Portal. In the Channel blade, select the direct-line icon (Figure 5-19).

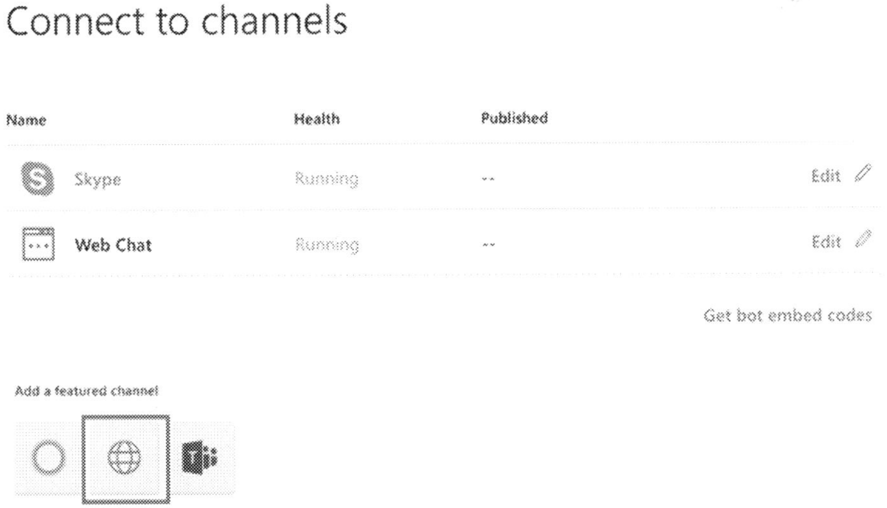

Connect to channels

Name	Health	Published	
Skype	Running	--	Edit
Web Chat	Running	--	Edit

Get bot embed codes

Add a featured channel

Figure 5-19. *Choose the direct-line icon from the Channel blade*

131

2. To configure a direct line, create a site that represents your client application, which will be connected to your chatbot. To do this, click "Add new site" (Figure 5-20) and name it.

Configure Direct Line

Figure 5-20. *Create a new site*

3. After creating the site, the Microsoft Bot Framework generates secret keys to be used by the client application to authenticate the direct-line API request, which is issued by the application to interact with your chatbot. Click Show for the corresponding key to view a key in plain text (Figure 5-21).

Configure Direct Line

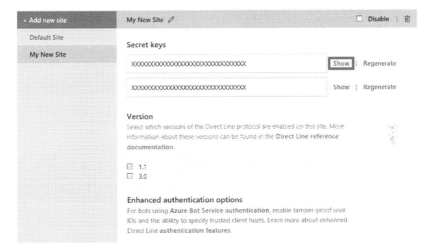

Figure 5-21. *Secret keys*

4. Copy and store the key that is shown (Figure 5-22) and use it to authenticate direct-line API requests that your client issues to communicate with your chatbot.

Configure Direct Line

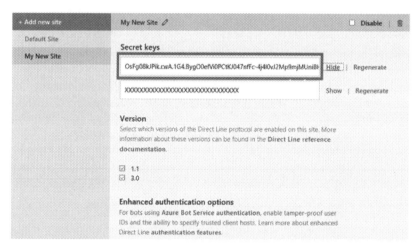

Figure 5-22. *Secret key to authenticate direct-line API requests*

5.   Last, open Azure Portal, click the Channel blade,
     and click the direct-line icon. Use the direct-
     line reference the client application will use to
     communicate with your chatbot. You can repeat
     this process, beginning with "Add new site," for each
     client application that you want to connect to your
     Chatbot.

As seen in Figure 5-19, which shows the Get Embed Code option, you
can use embedded code for configuration purposes. If you refer back to
Figure 5-20, you can set the size of `<iframe>` with `'width'` and `'height'`
tags or add a class to position and size the frame with cascading style
sheets. Secret keys can be used, as seen in Figure 5-23.

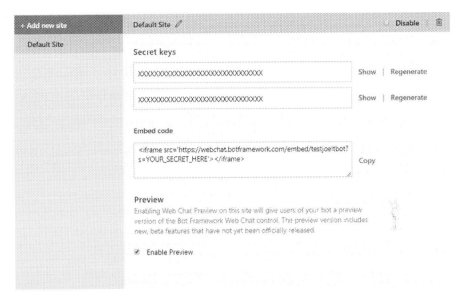

Figure 5-23. *Configuration using embedded code*

Connecting a Chatbot to Office 365 E-mail

Chatbots can be connected with Office 365 e-mail, similar to other communication channels. If you configure your chatbot to connect to e-mail, then the chatbot has multiple capabilities, such as sending notifications when new mail arrives in a mailbox, setting up predefined decline responses to meetings if there is conflict, and so on. To connect your chatbot to Office 365 e-mail, follow these steps:

1. Open the e-mail channel in Azure Portal, click the Channel blade for the e-mail.

2. Enter Office 365 credentials in the e-mail channel configuration (Figure 5-24).

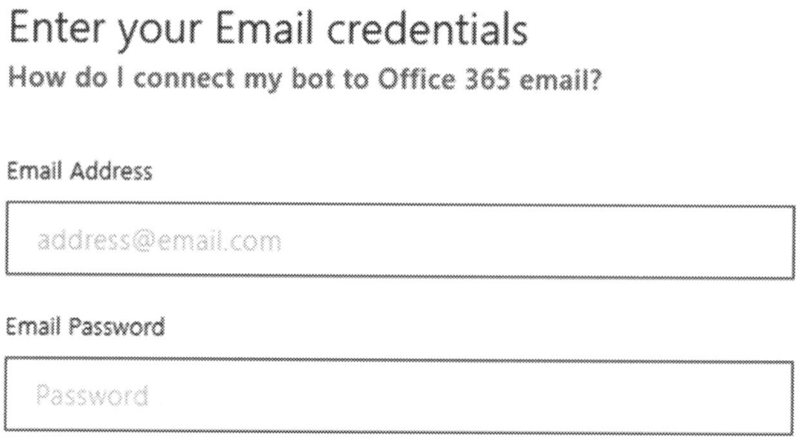

Enter your Email credentials
How do I connect my bot to Office 365 email?

Email Address

address@email.com

Email Password

Password

Figure 5-24. *Connect your bot to your Office 365 e-mail account*

3. The e-mail channels support custom sending properties to create customized replies. You can delineate HTML as the body of the message, indicate a subject for the e-mail subject line, assign importance to highlight e-mail priority, and add recipients in the TO, CC, and BCC fields using a semicolon as a separator.

Connecting a Chatbot to Facebook

To configure a chatbot to communicate with Facebook Messenger, enable Messenger on a Facebook page and connect it with the chatbot:

1. Create a new Facebook page or use an existing page. Go to the About Us page and copy and save the page ID. Then, create a Facebook app on the page and generate an app ID and an app secret ID for it. Insert the display name and contact e-mail for communication (Figure 5-25), then click Create App ID.

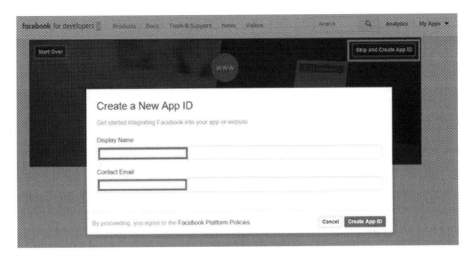

Figure 5-25. *Generate an app ID and an app secret ID*

2. Copy the generated app ID and app secret ID, and save them to the basic settings section (Figure 5-26).

Figure 5-26. *Copy and save the app ID and app secret ID*

3. Select the Advanced option and move the Allow API
    Access to App Settings slider to Yes (Figure 5-27).

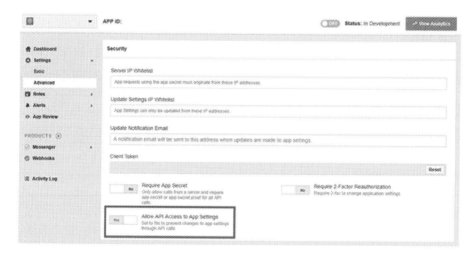

Figure 5-27. *Allow API access*

4. Then, enable Facebook Messenger in the new
    Facebook app by clicking Set Up in the Messenger
    blade (Figure 5-28).

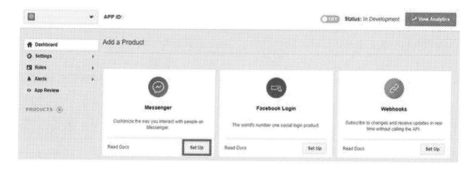

Figure 5-28. *Enable Facebook Messenger*

5. Under Settings, in the Token Generation screen, select the target page to generate an access token (Figure 5-29). Copy the token and save it temprorily, so that it can used in Figure 5-34.

Figure 5-29. *Access token for Facebook app*

6. To enable Webhooks to forward messaging events from Facebook Messenger to your chatbot, click Setup Webhooks (Figure 5-30).

Figure 5-30. *Set up Webhooks*

7. Now go to Azure Portal and, under Channels, click the Facebook Messenger icon. From there, copy the callback URL and verification token for the Facebook URL to the Webhook setup (Figure 5-31).

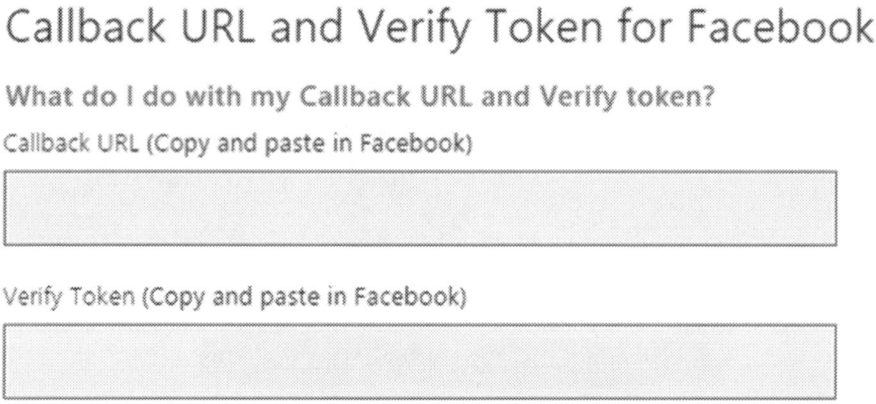

Callback URL and Verify Token for Facebook

What do I do with my Callback URL and Verify token?

Callback URL (Copy and paste in Facebook)

Verify Token (Copy and paste in Facebook)

Figure 5-31. *Callback URL and verification token for Facebook*

For a Webhook to subscribe to the Facebook page, go to the Facebook page and copy and paste the callback URL and the verification token for the Facebook values in New Page Subscription. In Subscription Fields, select messages, message_ deliveries, messaging_postbacks, and messaging_ options. Click Verify and Save (Figure 5-32).

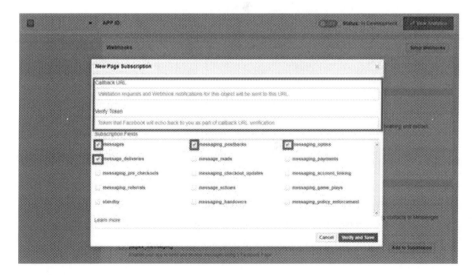

Figure 5-32. *New-page subscription setup*

8. Now go to the Webhooks setup page and select the
    page you created for the Webhook to subscribe to
    the Facebook page (Figure 5-33).

Figure 5-33. *Subscribe Webhooks to the Facebook page*

9. Log in to Azure Portal, choose Channel, and click
    the Facebook Messenger icon. Then, enter the
    Facebook app ID, the Facebook app secret ID,
    the page ID, and the page access token values
    copied earlier from Facebook Messenger. Multiple
    Facebook pages can use the same chatbot by adding
    additional page IDs and access tokens.

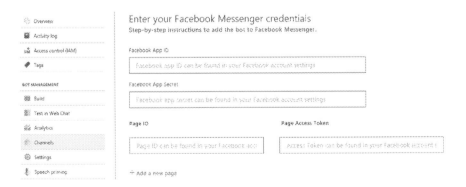

Figure 5-34. *Enter Facebook Messenger credentials*

To publish to the chatbot, it has go through the Facebook review and approval process. In general, Facebook requires a privacy policy URL and Terms of Service URL on its basic app settings page. To create a privacy policy, go to third-party resource links in the Code of Conduct page. The Terms of Use page contains sample terms to create a relevant Terms of Service document. For the review process to start, publish changes made to Facebook Messenger. The chatbot will be tested to ensure it is compliant with Facebook policies. When approved, in the App dashboard under App Review, set the app to Public. Ensure the Facebook page associated with this chatbot is published. Status appears in the Pages setting.

Connect a Chatbot to Facebook Workplace

To connect a chatbot with a workplace Facebook account, you need to create a custom integration:

1. Click the Admin Panel tab of Facebook at Workplace. Click Integrations and then click Create Custom Integration (Figure 5-35).

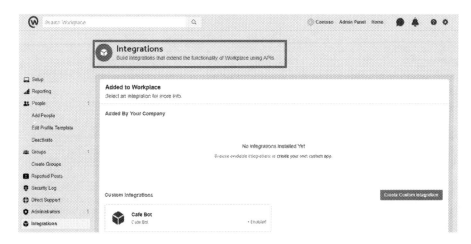

Figure 5-35. *Go to the Admin Panel of Facebook at Workplace, click Open Integration, and click the Create Custom Integration.*

2. Enter a display name and profile picture for this app. Set Allow API Access to App Settings to Yes and then copy and store the app ID, app secret ID, and app token displayed onscreen (Figure 5-36).

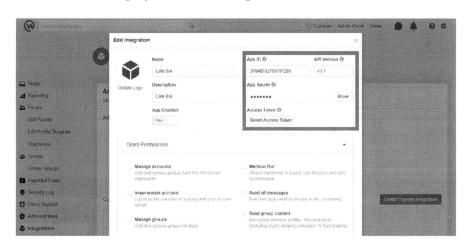

Figure 5-36. *In the workplace app, save the the app ID, app secret ID, and the app token.*

3. You now have a custom integration. You can find this page of type "Bot" in your workplace community, as shown in Figure 5-37.

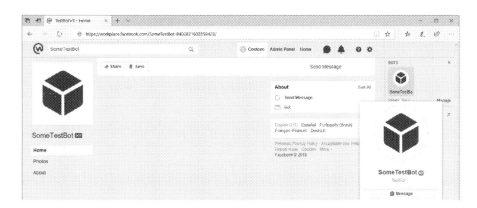

Figure 5-37. *Chatbot in a workplace community*

143

4. As before, log in to Azure Portal, paste the Facebook app ID, Facebook app secret ID, and page access token values (Figure 5-36). Use the numbers following the integration name on its About page, which is similar to the situation when we used the page ID from the About Us Facebook page.

5. Webhooks can be connected with the credentials shown in Azure in the case of Facebook Workplace. Submit for review and, when approved, Facebook Workplace is available for users. Publish the custom integration app and make it public, as we did earlier for Facebook.

Connect a Chatbot to GroupMe

To connect a chatbot to GroupMe, do the following:

1. Create an account in GroupMe. Complete the GroupMe application and use `https://groupme.botframework.com/Home/Login` as the callback URL (Figure 5-38).

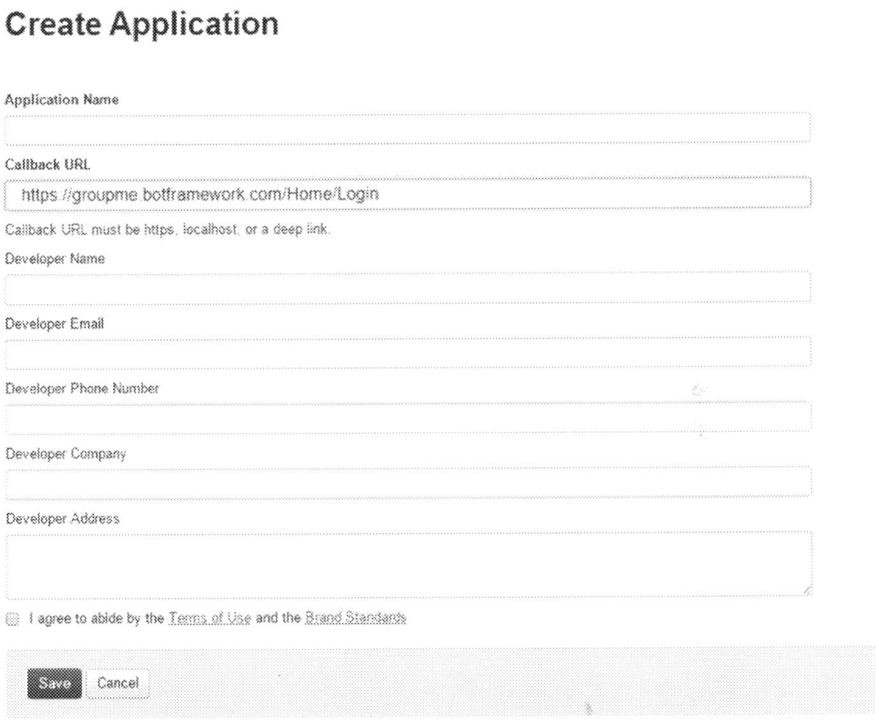

Create Application

Application Name

Callback URL

https //groupme botframework com/Home/Login

Callback URL must be https, localhost, or a deep link.

Developer Name

Developer Email

Developer Phone Number

Developer Company

Developer Address

☐ I agree to abide by the Terms of Use and the Brand Standards

[Save] Cancel

Figure 5-38. *Complete the GroupMe application*

2. Copy your client ID in Redirect URL and your access token as shown in Figure 5-39.

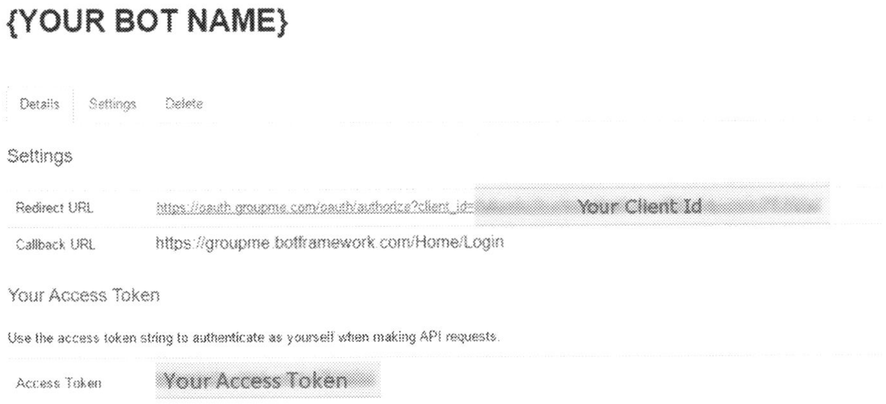

{YOUR BOT NAME}

Details | Settings | Delete

Settings

Redirect URL   https://oauth groupme com/oauth/authorize?client_id=   Your Client Id

Callback URL   https://groupme botframework com/Home/Login

Your Access Token

Use the access token string to authenticate as yourself when making API requests.

Access Token   Your Access Token

Figure 5-39. *Update credentials*

3. In dev.botframework.com, paste the access token
    into the Access Token field and the client ID into the
    Client ID field (Figure 5-40). Click Save to enable the
    chatbot.

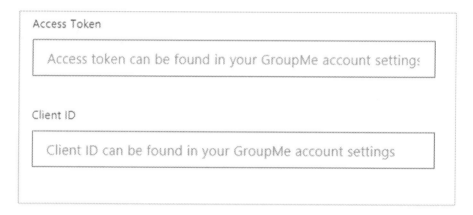

Figure 5-40. Readying the chatbot for publication

Summary

With this, we have come to the end of this chapter. We saw how easy it is
to connect an Azure chatbot to Cortana, Skype, Telegram Messenger, the
Kik messaging app, a direct line, Office 365 e-mail, Facebook Messenger,
Facebook Workplace, and GroupMe. In the next chapter, we examine the
benefits of using Azure chatbots.

CHAPTER 6

Business Benefits of Using Chatbots

This chapter is dedicated to studying the business benefits of Azure chatbots by exploring different advantages of chatbots. We also look at measures used to demonstrate business benefits of chatbots. First, we examine some interesting statistics on chatbots to get a sense of their significance, before looking at the details of business benefits.

Modern technology is not always adopted uniformly by countries. Variations are observed from country to country, and this is more likely linked to the culture associated with users in particular areas of a country. During the past five years, ordering food using chatbots has become prevalent in the United States. However, in India, it took some time before chatbots were adopted by large food chains such as MacDonald's, KFC, and others. In the United States, large enterprises are not the only ones using chatbots; small businesses are using chatbots in their day-to-day business operations as well. The statistics in Figure 6-1 (`collect.chat`) are based on data collected from August 2017 to January 2019. The figure depicts the top five countries where people regularly use chatbots.

© Charles Waghmare 2019
C. Waghmare, *Introducing Azure Bot Service*,
https://doi.org/10.1007/978-1-4842-4888-1_6

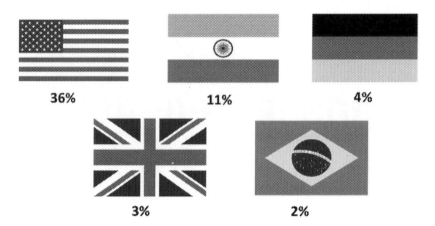

Figure 6-1. *Percentage of the population in different countries using chatbots*

As expected, the United States has made it to the top of the list. Following the United States, there is healthy competition coming from India, which is second on the list. India has the world's second highest number of Internet users. Organizations are confident about using chatbots and they are fully harnessing the potential chatbots hold. Chatbots can be translated into any language. Germany is in third place, followed by the United Kingdom and Brazil. Not shown in Figure 6-1 are Spain, France, Canada, Italy, Australia, and the United Arab Emirates—all of which are similarly ranked.

Figure 6-2 shows the top five industries currently profiting from chatbots. The data for the figure (`collect.chat`) were collected from August 2017 to January 2019. As we can see, real estate businesses use chatbots to the maximal extent (28%), followed by the travel industry (16%), education (14%), healthcare (10%), and finance (5%).

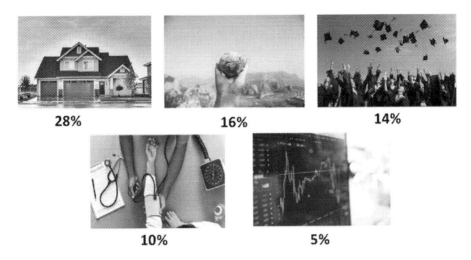

28%   **16%**   **14%**

10%   **5%**

Figure 6-2. *Industries that use chatbots*

One of the primary reasons chatbots are performing well in the real estate industry is because they generate plenty of leads. Chatbots today are widely adopted to produce leads, which is a necessity in the real estate industry. If there are no leads, there is nothing to sell.

The next industry on the list is the travel industry, which uses chatbots to answer user queries related to travel, thereby speeding up the travel booking process. A 24/7, 365-day presence of chatbots ensures that questions are addressed. The adoption of chatbots in education helps students engage in online courses, and helps students and parents complete the university admittance process. In the healthcare industry, chatbots are used to book appointments with doctors and diagnostic centers. Financial institutions are using chatbots to conduct preassessments and consultations with potential prospects.

Advantages of Chatbots

So far in this book, we have seen the benefits of chatbots for users and briefly covered business benefits. My primary objective in this section is to expand on that material and show how chatbots support and scale businesses to satisfy customers. Let's look at the benefits of chatbots (Figure 6-3) in business.

Figure 6-3. *Chatbot benefits*

Availability

Think about the occasions when you were required to wait several minutes before you could connect with a customer care representative to fix your issues, be they credit card related or insurance related, for example. There are then several minutes of waiting before your queries are actually resolved, which may be a painful experience. With chatbots, however, the waiting is over. Users can connect with chatbots whenever they want, in real time, to fix their issues. Chatbots are available 24/7, 365 days a year. They never get tired; they do not require breaks. They just continue to obey your commands and provide best-in-class user experiences. Some organizations have adopted smart chatbots, which means you can command them using speech and they will follow your orders.

Capacity Management

In the case of a call center, humans can communicate with one human at a time; the agent assists only one human caller. But with chatbots, this is a different story because they are able to communicate with multiple users. Regardless of the time of day or the number of people engaged in conversations with the chatbot, chatbots find answers immediately. There is no capacity constraint when it comes to chatbots.

Think about a restaurant that is famous for the quality of its food. In the evening, customer demand is high. It can be stressful to take food orders from customers manually, and sometimes restaurants are forced to deny certain orders because of capacity. However, when this restaurant starts using a chatbot, it is able to accept as many preorders and orders that it can, and serves its customers with greater satisfaction. If a customer orders a food item and that menu option is not available, the chatbot informs the customer immediately of the unavailability. Large food chains such as MacDonald's, Wendy's, Burger King, and Taco Bell have already installed chatbots to receive customer orders, and serve food with greater pride, independent of capacity.

Flexibility

When people move from one type of industry to another, they need to undergo training and acquire experience before they can start helping customers address their issues. This process takes time, and there is a monetary cost associated with it. The results may not guarantee success because employees may leave a company. In the case of chatbots, you can develop and design them so they can be used in any type of industry.

This is possible by changing conversation flows with the use of relevant words connected to a database. Here the results are guaranteed, because chatbots cannot "quit." When they are developed and designed, keeping the industry in mind, chatbots are all set to hit the floor and create a difference in your business. Chatbots are able to manage two-way conversations, which are quite prevalent in the customer service and retail industries. You can design chatbots that are aligned to industry type.

Greater User Experience

Humans are full of emotions and, sometimes, when addressing a customer with fairly large expectations, may affect the user experience negatively. Also, human-to-human interactions are bound to lead to conflict, most often requiring escalation to an upper echelon of people to tackle the situation. With chatbots, it is easy to manage customers of any type because chatbots are programmed to respond to customers based on the information fed to them and the rules built in them. Chatbots entertain customers with high, medium, and low expectations by meeting their requirements. Humans always prefer to have engaging conversations. When ordering from a restaurant for home delivery, a chatbot can give recommendations from previous orders, find your delivery address, and provide information on discounts and deals. The user is supersatisfied while placing the order, and the conversation is simple and engaging.

Low Cost

There are costs attached to hiring, training, and onboarding employees. In addition, the employee may not able to manage two or more customers at one time because the work is fairly complex, which may compromise the user experience. If an employee is unable to meet a sales target, this affects the business. Once developed, chatbots are able to engage thousands of customers at the same time, and users can jump into the conversation if they need to do so. Chatbots require a minimal development cost compared with hiring thousands of employees to support thousands of customers. One chatbot is able to serve thousands of customers with greater satisfaction and meet a monthly target. Even if targets are not met, there is not much of a business impact, but there are conversation trends, and organizations will have the opportunity to program chatbots in a new way to assist customers.

Faster Onboarding

If one is to accomplish a task with success, then one must train oneself or learn how to execute a task in the most efficient way to benefit an organization. Chatbots can help with the onboarding process Continuous training and teaching are involved at every level of the employee hierarchy that employees have to go through.

Employees come and go; this is a natural fact of business. Therefore, new employees must be trained. Companies want this to occur quickly; they want their people "up and running" as soon as possible so they are assets to the company. There is a greater possibly with chatbots that they could completely eliminate onboarding time, providing clear and easy-to-understand conversation flows with new employees. There is absolutely no doubt that there will be dynamic changes in chatbots too, but they will take little of your time to resolve compared to human employees.

Work Automation

Normally, people tend to get less productive when they are assigned to jobs that are repetitive. In general, we humans usually get bored by performing the same task over and over again. Chatbots have the capability of overcoming repetitive tasks by making them automated and executing them whenever they are required. There are already various Slack chatbots that are able to automate repetitive tasks, and this helps people save time and energy, and be more productive when coping with challenging tasks. Consider a situation in which you purchased an item and found it to be defective. You want to replace the item. There are e-commerce chatbots that do this with a single click. In addition, users can share images of the defective item with the vendor. There are smart financial chatbots that can inform you when there is flotation in stocks. There are smart chatbots that act as travel agents and are capable of booking your travel with a single click. There are two popular AI-based chatbots that have automated doctors' work: Dr. A.I. by HealthTap and Melody by Baidu.

New Sales Channels

Today, chatbots are able to sell products online because they're online 24/7, 365 days a year. In fact, during holidays, they are superbusy selling products because people connect to e-commerce sites more often during holidays. Per recent studies (chatbotsmagazine.com),
in the digital world, 70% of people prefer texting (read: using a chatbot) rather than calling and placing an order. Because of the dominance of Amazon in e-commerce, there is no need to drive to the mall and make a purchase. You can find almost anything online and buy items with one click. Chatbots always have an opportunity to sell products based on the needs of each customer. Chatbots are capable of remembering a customer's answers and can tailor their responses accordingly. By doing this, chatbots provide a personal touch and personal level of service that closely mirror human interaction.

E-commerce brands such as H&M, eBay shopbot, and Tommy Hilfiger are now selling their products using chatbots. Amazon has voice recognition AI (called *Alexa*) that is currently gaining in popularity.

Personal Assistance

Nowadays, people are able to use chatbots as personal fashion advisors to get recommendations for clothing, as financial advisors to request trading tips, as travel agents to suggest places to visit, as medical receptionists to book a doctor's appointment, as a source of entertainment to book movie tickets, and on and on. As mentioned earlier in this book, by using personas, chatbots are able to store choices and offer relevant options the next time you visit. One well-know chatbot is the CNN chatbot, which helps users receive personalized news (Trim). In addition, a personal finance chatbot, Taylor, is a travel assistant.

At Maruti Techlabs, there exists a requirement-gathering chatbot, Specter, designed using the Microsoft Bot Framework. The objective of designing such a chatbot was to assist the sales and marketing teams in improving efficiency when sharing requirements. Normally, Specter asks users a few questions to understand their requirements. It then forwards the information to the technical team, which validates and qualifies the lead. This saves hours of going back and forth with different teams during meetings, e-mail exchanges, and telephone calls.

Disadvantages of Chatbots

So far, we have looked at the advantages of chatbots. Let's check out some disadvantages as well:

- *Inability to understand:* As a result of using static programs to design chatbots, sometimes they may get stuck if an unprogrammed question is asked by a user. This leads to a poor customer experience and creates loss. Sometimes, multiple messaging can also tax users and worsen the overall customer experience.

- *Complex interface:* Chatbots are perceived as very complicated identities that requires plenty of time to comprehend user requirements.

- *Increased installation cost:* As we seen so far, chatbots are pretty useful in helping you save a lot in terms of manual human effort by ensuring 24/7 availability and by being able to serve multiple clients at once. But, unlike humans, every chatbot is required to be programmed differently based on business needs, which often change, which then leads to increased installation costs. Furthermore, there is also an increase in the time needed to develop and deploy an updated program, and this should be planned with minimal impact on the business and on customers. There may be last-minute changes too. Therefore, additional development requirements will increase costs.

- *Time-consuming:* Most of the time, the primary objective in deploying chatbots is to accelerate user response and create a better customer interaction and user experience. But, as a result of limitations such as data availability and the time required for a chatbot to self-update, any particular process is more time-consuming and expensive.

- *Zero decision making:* It is evident that chatbots cannot make smart decisions as humans do. They are known for their infamous inability to make decisions. One large company experienced a situation in which its chatbot went on a racist rant. It is critical to manage the precise programing of your chatbot to prevent incidents that may affect your sales and reputation negatively.

- *Poor memory:* Until we create personas in the background, which requires some additional investment, chatbots do not have the capability of memorizing past conversations, which forces users to retype the same conversation again and again. This can be extremely annoying for users. Therefore, it is important to be diligent while designing chatbots and ensure that programs are able to comprehend user queries and react accordingly.

To summarize, although chatbots are our future, we have yet to uncover their full potential. Their rising popularity means they will stay in the market for a long time. Machine learning has transformed the way companies communicate with their customers. Along with new technology platforms supporting the Microsoft Bot Framework, new types of chatbots are being developed. It is exciting to experience the development of a new domain in technology while surpassing previous ones.

Define Success Metrics for an Azure Chatbot

We have come to the last part of this chapter. Here, we define metrics that can be used to measure the success of Azure chatbots. A metric is a quantifiable measure used to track and assess the status of a specific business process and scope for improvement. Defining metrics is important because their use measures the success of a chatbot, and a return on investment can be calculated. For newly created chatbots, some of the metrics may not be applicable until the chatbot has been in use for a while. Companies need to monitor metrics closely. Most of the time, expectations for chatbots are greater conversion, efficiency, and faster response as they engage users. Companies must define the right metrics based on these key parameters. In this way, the performance of the chatbot can be monitored to improve its efficiency.

User Metrics

There are different types of metrics. Let's start with defining user metrics (Figure 6-4):

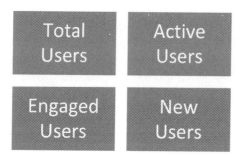

Figure 6-4. *User metrics*

- *Total users:* Total users is the most basic metric. It records the number of people using your chatbot. This measure is important because trends and patterns will reflect a change in the number of users and the amount of data to which the chatbot has been exposed. This metric also provides critical information about market size, which may affect your chatbot.

- *Active users:* The active users metric identifies the number of people who are able to read messages in the chatbot during conversations with users. Active users are potential targets for the success of a chatbot. The potential effects of a promotional campaign can be estimated from the number of active users. The number of people who read your message is absolutely critical. User engagement is not guaranteed, but the content is seen by users.

- *Engaged users:* The engaged users metric identifies the number of users who enter into a conversation with a chatbot. They send and receive messages. The engaged user statistics is important because the chatbot will be able to provide the conversation statistics. This kind of metric definitely shapes decisions regarding the effectiveness of the chatbot. It will be pretty evident when a chatbot is unable to start a conversation with users.

- *New users:* The new users metric captures the new set of users who saw messages in your chatbot after a promotional campaign. This metric is necessary to keep a count of active users. Customer preferences change over time, and the number of interactions with the chatbot may decline. For this reason, there is a need to have new users to keep your customer base strong.

Message Metrics

The next type of metric we examine is message metrics (Figure 6-5).

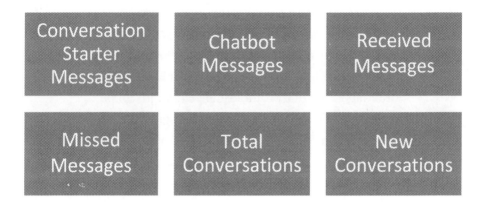

Figure 6-5. Message metrics

The following metrics capture trends in your overall user base and provide details on how users interact with your chatbot:

- *Conversation starter messages:* Conversation starter messages are those kicked off by users, not the chatbot. This metric includes the total number of messages initiated by a user while starting a conversation with a chatbot. This figure is important for determining the organic growth of the chatbot. When a user initiates a conversation with a message, the chatbot can send a message to acknowledge the user message. However, companies work to reduce the number for this metric because it is more effective if the chatbot starts the conversation. When a business implements a chatbot for customer relations management or digital marketing, after an initial greeting is sent by the chatbot, it needs to continue to send messages to keep the user engaged.

- *Chatbot messages:* The chabot messages metric includes the total number of messages sent by the chatbot during a conversation with the user. Other chatbot message information helps to measure the length of a conversation between a customer and the chatbot. In general, we want this number of messages to be high. But, the chatbot needs to adhere to one critical condition: send accurate messages during a user conversation. We have seen bad chatbot implementations when the bot cannot understand the user input. In these cases, the chatbot replies with similar words repeatedly.

- *Received messages:* The received messages metric identifies the number of messages sent by a user during a conversation with the chatbot. With this metric, we can assess whether the user was engaged with the chatbot. If this value is low, we don't need a chatbot. Ideally, in social media platforms such as Facebook and Twitter, this will make more sense and minimal sense using a chatbot living in Facebook or WhatsApp.

- *Missed messages:* The missed messages metric is the total number of messages the chatbot could not process based on user input. This metric may be hard to calculate. The reason for not processing a request could be because the input string entered by the user was in a language the chatbot does not understand.

- *Total conversations:* As its name suggests, the total conversations metric is the total number of conversations started and completed successfully on a given day. This leads to engaged users.

- *New conversations:* Also as its name suggests, the new conversations metric is the total number of new conversations started. It includes conversations involving inexperienced users and those conversations initiated by returning users on a different matter.

Performance Metrics

Now let's look at metrics critical for measuring the performance of a chatbot:

- *Retention rate:* The retention rate metric is defined as the percentage of users that returns to use the chatbot in a given time frame. This measurement is important because we need to keep customers engaged to extract insights related to their preferences by creating situations that make them spend maximal time engaging with a chatbot. Using these preferences, personas for each user are created and reused by the chatbot to respond to similar queries made by other users. High retention rates can be achieved by promotional campaigns, such as engaging with a chatbot to receive a 50% discount or guess a word to receive an exciting prize. These retention strategies can be achieved by a high-quality chatbot capable of meeting—and exceeding—customer expectations. Figure 6-6 shows a sample retention rate printout.

	Day 1	Day 2	Day 3	Day 4	Day 5	Day 6	Day 7	
September 9	58%	64%	38%	12%	96%	97%	48%	0
September 10	92%	123%	16%	32%	98%	85%	31%	25
September 11	67%	35%	19%	88%	88%	30%	114%	50
							Number of People: 4700	
September 12	24%	35%	114%	115%	44%	32%	47%	75
September 13	8%	48%	132%	117%	13%	82%	84%	100
September 14	19%	117%	72%	8%	120%	1%	64%	125
September 15	10%	78%	52%	5%	6%	31%	123%	150

Figure 6-6. *Sample retention rate printout*

- *Goal completion rate (GCR):* The GCR is used to record the total percentage of successful engagements executed using a chatbot. For an e-commerce B2B or B2B2C company, chatbot metrics on GCR reveal level information percolated to user related to products or its purchasing details. This metric also reveals the number of times the chatbot has processed user input successfully and provided the requested information. We can also do data mining over questions asked by the users. The metric is used to identify overall trends in consumer preferences (personas) to calculate the GCR. In Figure 6-7, we see a graph of phrases uttered by users. The graph clearly shows how users are engaging with the chatbot to schedule rides. Hence, greater focus should be placed on this issue to keep the consumer engaged and active.

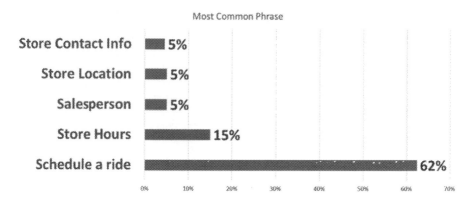

Figure 6-7. *GCR of users scheduling a ride*

- *Goal completion time or messages:* As discussed several times in this book, chatbots need to provide efficient services and good user experiences; otherwise, there are plenty of chatbot substitutes, such as web pages or apps. Effort reduction to complete a goal can improve the user experience, which can be achieved in many ways. One way is to provide relevant answers to user queries on time.

- *Fallback rate (FBR):* No chatbot is perfect. It may fail because it cannot process user inputs, because of a design issue and so on. The FBR is the percentage of times the chatbot failed to process user input. A greater FBR indicates improvement is needed in the chatbot; a low FBR indicates better chatbot efficiency. This metric is very useful in the customer service industry, such as at help desks or call centers, where chatbots are expected to provide accurate information based on user input.

- *User satisfaction:* The user satisfaction metric can be measured through exit surveys. At the end of a conversation, users can be prompted to rate their experience: Did this chatbot do well? Include a binary answer of yes or no. This metric helps companies understand the overall effectiveness of a chatbot as rated by the user.

- *Virality:* The virality metric calculates whether an existing user was motivated by the chatbot to include other users in the conversation.

Summary

With this, we have now come to the end of this chapter. We looked at some important statistics regarding chatbots. We also examined the advantages and disadvantages of chatbots. Last, we looked at metrics for measuring the success of chatbots. In the next chapter, we look at creating new solutions using Azure chatbots.

CHAPTER 7

Create Solutions Using Chatbots

In this chapter, we focus on how we can create solutions using chatbots and look at some best use cases of chatbots. The objective of this chapter is to bring insight to how chatbots are valuable solutions in a variety of situations, such as automating the password reset process, rendering a knowledgeable response, and searching for information. Chatbots are used as solutions to business problems across industries—from call centers to medical practices, from banking to insurance, from IT to manufacturing.

Utility Service Providers

Chatbots can be deployed by utility services such as electric, gas, and water providers to meet customer requirements on time and with satisfaction. With these types of services, customers often raise questions regarding the service, and queries need to be addressed accurately and in a timely manner. In case of a gas bill, consumers often ask why the consumption for the current month is more than the previous month. With regard to the electric bill, consumers might ask why, despite being on holiday for a couple weeks, the electrical bill did not go down. For water services, customers might inquire why the water pressure has been reduced for the past few weeks. To ask these questions, consumers send e-mail, Short Message Services (SMS), write letters, or make phone calls. However, it takes some time before their query is answered.

But with the evolution of chatbots, things have changed. Consumer queries are answered instantly. During real-time conversations, chatbots are able to query the consumer database in real time and provide accurate answers (Figure 7-1).

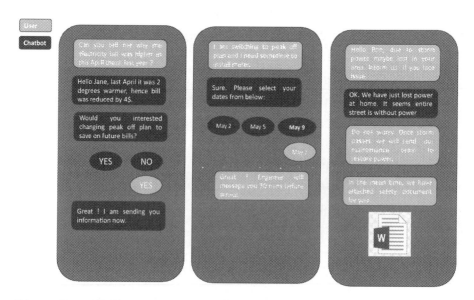

Figure 7-1. *Utility service provider chatbots*

The telecom industry is very competitive as a result of multiple service providers that often have very big targets to provide services such as the Internet with high-quality bandwidth but at a discounted rate; to retain customers with excellent service, such as 24/7, 365-day support, and no downtime; and providers even offer gifts under the guise of customer loyalty programs. In this class of service, most frequently asked queries from consumers are: Why is my Internet not working? How can I upgrade my current subscription? What is my account balance? Companies used to have call centers to manage customer service; but, today, chatbots are used to manage such tasks in an efficient way (Figure 7-2).

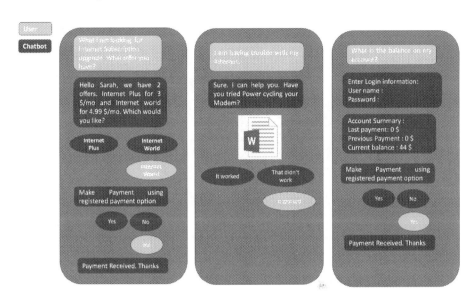

Figure 7-2. *Telcom industry chatbots*

Insurance Companies

Insurance companies around the world are constantly adopting different techniques to get more customers onboard and to retain existing ones. To do so, AI is being used to answer queries (Figure 7-3) such as: How do I file an accident claim? Does my policy cover workplace injuries? Does my existing policy cover my wife as well?

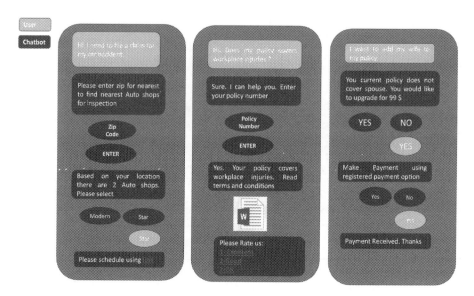

Figure 7-3. *Insurance company chatbots*

Travel Agencies

Travel agencies—and specifically the airline industry—are often misjudged by most passengers for miscommunicating departure and arrival data, and other details. Now, chatbots are the preferred method for communicating details of flights, for example, and other related information (Figure 7-4).

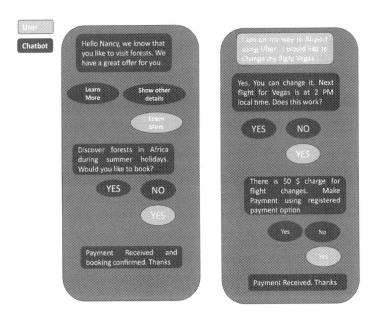

Figure 7-4. *Travel company chatbots*

Healthcare Industry

The healthcare industry has also adopted AI technologies to serve patients in a better way. Manual processes such as scheduling appointments, reminding patients of doctor follow-up appointments, and answering general queries on health-related matters can be done using chatbots (Figure 7-5).

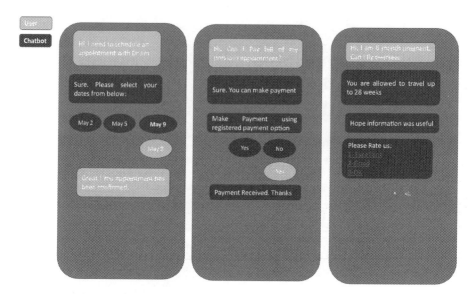

Figure 7-5. Healthcare industry chatbots

Financial Services

Using chatbots, digital banks have automated level 1 support, such as reissuing credit and debit cards; resetting account passwords; issuing checks; providing autodebit and bill-paying services; determining personal, mortgage, and vehicle loan eligibility; and more (Figure 7-6). Some banks, such as Citibank, have maximized their online operations and have limited the number of banks where customers can conduct their financial business. Banks such as HDFC have been performing credit card operations in an online manner.

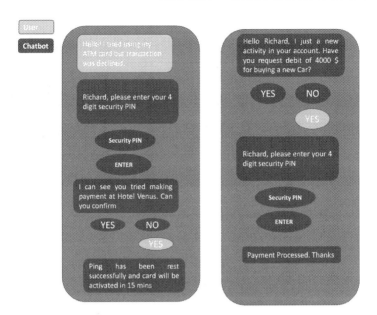

Figure 7-6. *Financial service provider chatbots*

Protection against Fraud

A chatbot can be used to detect fraud. For example, when a customer requests a PIN, the chatbot can be configured to request the customer to answer security questions. An online transaction password is then sent to the account holder's e-mail or through an SMS. When both of these are verified, the account holder can view the account and make transactions from it (Figure 7-7).

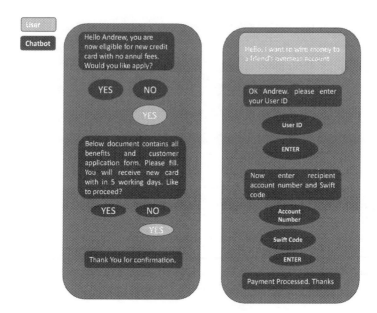

Figure 7-7. *Financial fraud detector chatbot*

If incorrect information is entered, the chatbot can inform the user of this and assign a human banker to assist.

Designing Solutions Using Azure Chatbots

In this section, we design solutions using Azure chatbots. Let's start with task automation. The task automation chatbot helps users perform single or multiple tasks without any assistance from human beings. This type of chatbot appears in web sites or mobile apps and communicate with users using rich user controls and text. Such chatbots are enabled with NLP understanding to build engaging conversations. Let's look at a password reset example.

Password Reset Use Case

To understand more fully the nature of a task bot, consider the following password reset use case. Nowadays, IT service departments get multiple requests for directions on how to reset a password. The task is simple to execute, and team members spend large amounts of time handling these mundane requests. This task can be managed easily using a chatbot. In the following exchange, Adam is the chatbot and Bobby is the user:

> Adam: Hello, Bobby! How can I can help you?
> Choose one option.
>
> Password reset | Need help desk contact number |
> Need LAN cable
>
> Bobby: Password reset
>
> Adam: You request has been processed successfully.
>
> Adam: Use Test123 as a temporary password. You
> will be asked to change your password after you
> have logged in using the temporary password.
>
> Adam: Have a good day.
>
> Bobby: Super!

Some might ask: If a chatbot resembles a mobile app or web site, why not just build the web site or mobile app instead of a chatbot? Building a mobile app or web site instead of a chatbot is a choice made by an organization. But, if you look at the situation from a design perspective and consider the amount of time and money required to develop the three options, chatbots are much cheaper and may not require a complex design. Furthermore, chatbots can be made available in a web site or mobile app to create a conversational experience with the user community. As mentioned previously, you can do this using the Microsoft

Bot Framework direct-line API or web chat control. Thus, chatbots are a simple way to resolve complex problems, such as resolve consumer queries in utility business; manage tasks efficiently in a 24/7, 365-day support services environment, help people file insurance claims with supporting information, get real-time details of flights during travel, schedule doctor appointments, answer health-related queries, reset passwords, and protect against fraud in financial services.

Embed a Chatbot in a Web Site

In general, chatbots reside outside web sites or mobile apps, but there are several examples when chatbots are embedded in web sites or mobile apps so that users can seek information in the most efficient way. Sometimes, as a result of the complex structure of a web site, users are unable to find the information they need. Using a chatbot, however, they can engage in a useful conversation to get information. As we have seen, chatbots can resolve simple issues and hand off more complex issues to human agents. In this section, we look at the integration between chatbots and web sites, and the process of using back-channel mechanisms to facilitate communication between chatbots and web pages. Microsoft provides two ways of integrating chatbots with web sites: Skype web control and an open source web control.

Skype Web Control

The Skype web control is essentially a Skype client in a web-enabled control. Built-in Skype authentication enables the bot to authenticate and recognize users without requiring the developer to write any custom code. Skype automatically recognizes Microsoft accounts used by its web client.

Skype web control acts as a front end for Skype, and the user's Skype client automatically accesses the full context of the conversation, facilitated by web control. Even after a browser is closed, the user may continue to interact with the chatbot using the Skype client.

Open Source Web Control

An open source web chat control is based on ReactJS and it uses a direct-line API to communicate with the Microsoft Bot Framework. The web chat control provides a blank canvas for implementing a web chat, allows full control over conversational behavior, and offers a good user experience. Through back-channel mechanisms, the web page hosting the control communicates directly with the chatbot, which is invisible to the user. This capability enables a number of useful scenarios. For example, the chatbot can send relevant data to the web page, such as the user profile, and can send commands to the web page.

Here are useful capabilities of web control:

- The web page can send relevant data, such as a GPS location, to the chatbot.

- The web page can advise a user to a perform an action, such as select an option from a drop-down menu.

- The web page can send an authorization token for the logged-in user

Back-channel Mechanism

As we just saw, an open source web chat control communicates with chatbots using a direct-line API, which allows an exchange of activities between the user and the chatbot. A common type of activity is messaging, and typing indicates that a user is typing or the chatbot is working to compile a response. A back-channel mechanism can be used effectively to exchange information between client or user and chatbot without actually presenting it to the user.

Embed a Chatbot Inside a Mobile App

Integrating a chatbot with a mobile app depends on the kind of mobile app we use. Check out the following:

- *Native mobile app:* A mobile app created using native code can communicate with the Microsoft Bot Framework using a direct-line API or by using the REST API or web sockets.

- *Web-based mobile app:* A mobile app built using web language and frameworks can communicate with the Microsoft Bot Framework using the same components as a chatbot embedded in a web site, which is encapsulated within a native app's shell.

IoT App

An IoT app can communicate with the Microsoft Bot Framework using a direct-line API. It can also use Microsoft Cognitive Services to enable capabilities such as image recognition and speech.

Design Knowledge Chatbots

Knowledge chatbots are chatbots that provide knowledge-based responses to user queries. What will be the weather in the city next week? Which is the nearest coffee shop to my house? Which hit film is available in the nearest movie theater? Does my credit card offer access to the lounge facility at the airport? If a chatbot is designed to answer these questions, it is a knowledge chatbot. Knowledge chatbots are smarter and more powerful compared to FAQ-based chatbots, which are designed to answer with predefined replies. Regardless of their design, chatbots pull information from various relational databases and present it to users in an understandable format.

Search Using Chatbots

The search functionality is a valuable asset for chatbots. A standard search provides accurate results based on the input string entered by a user. For example, if a user enters "India" in the search results, entries with a precise match and close match to India appear. If a user asks a knowledgeable chatbot for information on music by Impala, the chatbot responds with relevant information, as shown in Figure 7-8.

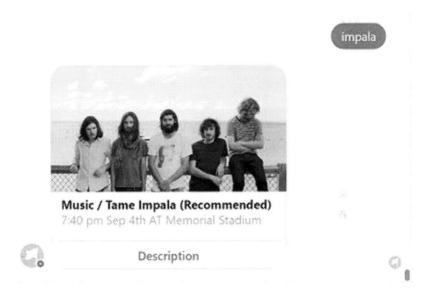

Figure 7-8. *Search result from a knowledge chatbot*

If the chatbot is unable to provide a precise match, it can present a result with the comment: "Here is the event that best matches your search" (Figure 7-9). Based on the accuracy of the search result, the chatbot can tailor communication while presenting results to the user.

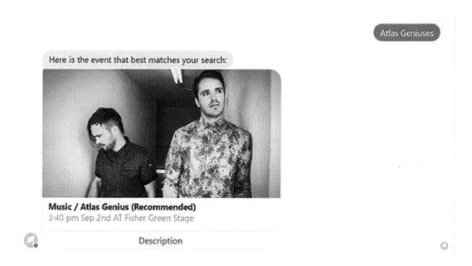

Figure 7-9. *Search result with a match that is not precise*

If there is no accurate or precise match, but a close match for a search string such as "confidence is low", then the chatbot may respond with the search result: Hmm . . . were you looking for any of these events? (Figure 7-10).

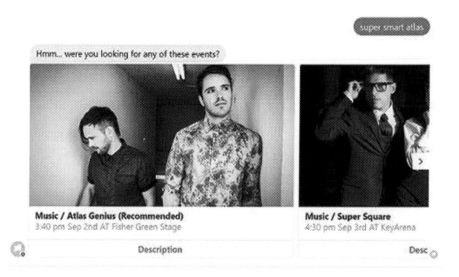

Figure 7-10. *Search result with low confidence*

Using Search to Guide a Conversation

If there is a motivation to build chatbots to enable basic search engine functionality only, then there is no requirement for a chatbot. A conversational interface offers multiple benefits that users cannot get from a typical search engine using a web browser.

Knowledge chatbots are most effective when they are designed to guide the conversation with a user. Conversation consists of an exchange between a user and a chatbot. During the conversation, the chatbot has the opportunity to ask questions, present options for selection, and validate outcomes, which a standard or basic search is incapable of doing. In Figures 7-11 though 7-14, the chatbot converses with a user using facets and filters until it locates the information requested by the user.

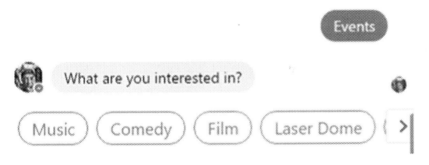

Figure 7-11. *Search result to guide user*

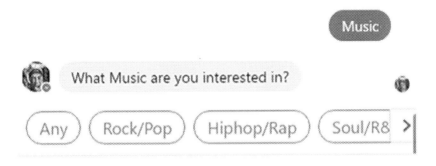

Figure 7-12. *Search result to guide user*

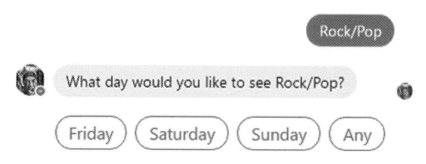

Figure 7-13. *Search result to guide user*

Figure 7-14. *Search result to guide user*

By processing the user's input and presenting relevant options during the conversation, the chatbot connects the user to the information being sought. After the chatbot delivers this information, it can also provide guidance on more efficient ways to find similar information in the future. Check out Figure 7-15.

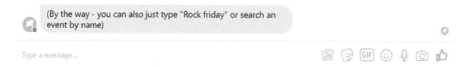

Figure 7-15. *Search result to guide user*

Azure Search

Azure chatbots can be enabled with Azure Search to create an efficient search index that a chatbot can easily search, facet, and filter. Figure 7-16 shows an example search index created using Azure Portal.

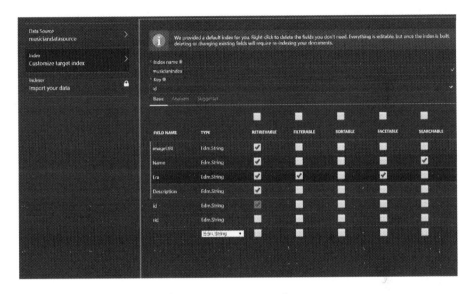

Figure 7-16. *Search index in Azure Portal*

To access all properties of the data store, set the property as "retrievable." You expect to find musicians by name, so set the Name property as "searchable." Last, you want to facet and filter over musicians' eras, so mark the Eras property as both "facetable" and "filterable." Faceting determines the values that exist in the data store for a given property. Figure 7-17 shows there are five distinct eras in the data store. Filtering returns only specified instances of a certain property. For example, you can filter the result set to contain only items where era is equal to "Romantic."

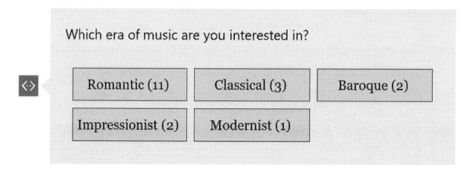

Figure 7-17. *Faceting values*

Transitioning Conversations from Bot to Human

In the last section of this chapter, we look at the situation when it is necessary to transition conversations from bot to human. Regardless of how smart you develop your chatbot using AI, cognitive services, and NLP, there are times where human intervention cannot be prevented.

Triage

In this situation, the chatbot provides a response to the user queries and later collects user data such as name, e-mail address, and any pertinent information related to the queries, then stores it in a database to transition conversation control to a human agent. Using a chatbot to triage information helps human agents work on the complex task to be addressed.

Escalation

Typically, in a help desk scenario, a chatbot may be able to answer basic questions and tend to trivial issues while performing simple operations such as resetting a user's password. However, in a situation when the user issue appears to be complex and the chatbot is unable to manage it, a human must intervene. In these situations, the chatbot must understand the set of issues it can fix and those it cannot fix and thus requires a human agent. There are multiple ways chatbots determine that they need to transfer control of the conversation to a human.

User-driven Menus

One of the simplest ways for chatbots to handle user dilemmas is to present users with a menu of options from which they can select. Tasks that the chatbot can handle independently appear in the menu, along with a link labeled "Chat with an agent." This implementation does not require advanced machine learning or natural language for understanding. The chatbot simply transfers control of the conversation to a human agent as soon as the user selects the "Chat with an agent" option.

Scenario Driven

The bot may decide to transfer control based on whether it determines it is capable of handling the scenario. The bot collects some information about the user's request and then queries its internal list of capabilities to determine whether it is capable of addressing that request. If the bot determines that it is capable of addressing the request, it does so; if the bot determines the request is beyond the scope of issues it can resolve, it transfers control of the conversation to a human agent.

Supervision

In some scenarios, human agents prefer to monitor the conversation between the user and the chatbot instead of taking control. In the situation of a help desk, where a chatbot is communicating with a user to diagnose a computer problem, a machine learning model helps the chatbot determine the most probable cause of the problem. However, before advising the user to take a specific course of action, the chatbot can privately confirm the identified diagnosis and solution with the human agent, and then proceed with authorization. When the human agent authorizes the solution, the chatbot presents the solution to the user. The chatbot is still performing the majority of the work, but the human agent retains control over the final decision.

Summary

With this, we come to the end of this chapter. We saw examples of chatbots being used in different industries. We also examined how chatbots can be used to automate processes such as resetting passwords, providing useful information, searching using chatbots, and searching with chatbots using information embedded in web sites or mobile apps. Last, we studied when chatbots need to transition conversations to human agents to address complex queries.

CHAPTER 8

Create Digital Transformation Using Chatbots

In this chapter, we create digital transformation using Azure chatbots with a focus on customer satisfaction. Digital transformation using Azure can be accomplished in various ways by using Azure products and services such chatbots, cloud storage, identity and access management, IoT, databases, DevOps, AI and machine learning, and a plethora of products. Digital transformation is the phase during which Azure products and services help to engage your customers, empower your employees, optimize your operation, and transform the user experience. Let's explore digital transformation using Azure chatbots.

Building the Customer Experience

In this section we look at different business scenarios in which customer experience is hailed by the use of chatbots. We see simple examples in which businesses have transformed themselves to offer a digital customer experience to end users.

© Charles Waghmare 2019
C. Waghmare, *Introducing Azure Bot Service*,
https://doi.org/10.1007/978-1-4842-4888-1_8

Digital Transformation: Corporate or Internal Communications Using "Truthbot"

One of the most powerful and underestimated departments in business is Internal Communications. These employees are required to do more with less—less budget and less people—but produce more work. These individuals are not always fortunate enough to have digital communication tools to conduct their tasks. They must rely on a predigital and centrally governed model for communication. Their ways of working are a direct contradiction to producing a digital customer experience. Nowadays, organizations are ready to spend money to offer a digital experience to their customers, but don't really bother about their employees, who are responsible for producing the digital customer experience. In short, organizations can offer a digital customer experience to their employees, which creates a direct positive impact, as well as provide the same or an enhanced digital experience to customers. It is high time for the director or chief of Internal Communications to revamp the corporate communication strategy, methodologies, and tools to align with the current revolution of digital transformation.

The existence of internal communication is to be the primary source of truth for all employees, sponsors, executives, and stakeholders. Internal Communications teams work collaboratively to publish truth in the most understandable way. Communication teams offer variation to their recipients by publishing news, information, and announcements on hot topics and trends so that readers find the knowledge useful. The result is user satisfaction. Some communications engage openly with employees and executives to generate topics on which they can publish information through an intranet.

In today's world, we all have digital personas produced by our online behavior and our interactions with different applications. Furthermore, these personas are produced using internal messaging platforms in the form of reviews or previews about products and services. In the digital world, our perceptions are built by what is trending on social media rather than what we perceive as important. Headlines gain more attention, news in the form of videos or animation generate more views and shares, and analyses in the news gain maximum visibility. These are a few of the new trends created by digital media that attempt to produce news and information in the way people expect in the digital world.

As we experience the era of digital transformation, huge efforts and investments are made to create natural human conversation between humans and machines, and this is witnessed in the development of chatbots. The adoption of chatbots has a conversational interface with branding, marketing, commerce, Internet searches, customer service, and perhaps even the Internet itself. Today, it is uncommon to see banners such as "Chat with us" when we open a web site or mobile app. With such progress there is a strong feeling that other personalized communication channels such as e-mail, web portals, or mobile apps are not able to be sustained in the digital transformation era.

Directors of Internal Communications channels should focus on revamping their strategy and create a new team of communicators that can create a digital transformation. Operationally, this implies the communicators function more as guardians of conversations, rather than agents of approved content. They should spend more time listening and moderating, rather than creating and modifying content both on internal and external company networks. Digitally transformed companies have a social media command center that monitors the posts and sentiments of their network, and produces a plan of action based on trends noted.

Employees prefer internal messaging platforms over corporate e-mail or intranets, and governance over these platforms is very limited. Internal Communications teams generally have the perception that such responsibility lies with the IT department.

For Internal Communications teams now, there is an opportunity for chatbots to create a source of truth using Truthbot, rather than follow a reactive approach to build products based on the sentiments of employees and stakeholders received through feedback and suggestions. Truthbot converses with employees and stakeholders 24/7, provides access to precise information, and listens to employee concerns based on conversational trends, and much more.

The implementation of Truthbot using an Azure chatbot is an omni-channel solution accessed by thousands of employees at once through multiple channels such as intranets, internal social collaboration platforms, Smart Messaging Services, and personal virtual assistant devices. It is powered by AI. Truthbot can ask questions as well as answer them. It can store user information to support data mining, and can identify patterns and trends to support future communications and facilitate decision making. Truthbot will emerge as a new source of employee insight. An AI-powered conversational user experience is the epitome of how Internal Communications employees can benefit from digital innovation. Imagine the following conversation with Truthbot to manage a rumor that is making its way through a company:

> Employee: Hello. Is there heavy snowfall in the city? Are the roads blocked?
>
> Truthbot: No, sir. The temperature is eight degrees centigrade and the sun is shining.
>
> Employee: Can I leave my office and drive home easily?
>
> Truthbot: Yes, sir. Please contact me whenever you have a question.

Just imagine if you have 1,000 employees and most of them ask the same question of the facility management team. This would create chaos. The Internal Communications team could use a chatbot to interact with employees who are worried about potentially hazardous driving conditions. Truthbot helps executives think about internal communications in a different way.

How Chatbots Are Improving the State of Healthcare in India

India has a profound history in healthcare that reaches back to 273 BC, when the study of medicine was flourishing. During the British reign, there were a lot of hospitals built in India. After achieving independence, large private hospitals were built that use modern technology for treatment. However, the cost of medical treatment has always been on the high side in private hospitals; but, in government hospitals, despite less money being spent on treatment, medical services lack resources. Despite this, there are multiple chains of private hospitals that offer best-in-class service. Adoption of technology has changed the way treatment, disease control, research and development, and paramedical services are conducted and delivered. It has also saved time and money, and provided better accessibility to more people. In fact, people from other countries visit India to avail themselves of the healthcare facilities there.

mHealth is an abbreviation for mobile health—a term used for the practice of medicine and public health supported by mobile devices. An article published by the Singapore Healthcare Management Congress (www.singaporehealthcaremanagement.sg) indicates that, currently, healthcare has been transformed into the digital healthcare term "mHealth." According to the article, 59% of people say that mHealth has changed how they find information on health issues; 49% say they expect mHealth to change how they manage their overall health. Wearable technology used to track health status has a market value of $3.1 billion. Technology giants such as Microsoft, Google, Apple, and Samsung are continuously in quest of developing healthcare products and services that can be adopted by users. There has also been a tremendous increase in the field of AI and nanotechnology during the past few decades in the healthcare sector. With the introduction of AI such as chatbots, it is evident that healthcare depends on technology for its progress.

There are plenty of chatbots available, such as your.md, sensely, buoy health, and infermedica, that help people gain confidence by providing them with useful and accurate results about their health. This shows how technology is changing the healthcare industry and making our lives better. These chatbots have successfully helped millions of people across the globe in addressing their health issues and giving proper advice. There are countless examples where AI can help doctors, nurses, and patients attain better healthcare, but it requires proper implementation.

The big hospitals in India, such as Lilavati Hospital, Fortis Hospital, Apollo Speciality Hospital, Hinduja, Breach Candy, and Saifee Hospital, are using chatbots to engage patients with their hospital. The chatbots live on web sites and mobile apps, and touch screens are available in these hospitals. The chatbots help visitors access information related to the hospital, such as medical departments, the pharmacy, doctors, careers, appointment booking, and a lot more. Furthermore, chatbots are capable of understanding user queries related to appointments, careers, medicine, disease, diet, billing, services, and more, and they can reply accordingly. This helps hospitals save a lot of customer support time. Manual tasks are automated, which not only saves time and money, but also is considered an advancement in India's healthcare sector. Here are a few of the tasks that are best performed by chatbots in a healthcare setting.

- Schedule appointments with doctors.

- Respond to general user queries related to hospitals or doctors.

- Send reminders to patients.

- Identify a patient's illness based on the symptoms entered.

- Build patient engagement.

Each year, the Indian government launches plenty of healthcare schemes, so that the state of healthcare improves in India, which affects lower and middle-class families. Chatbot implementations in healthcare reveal to us how chatbots are improving healthcare status in India. They help to increase reliability and reduce the cost of healthcare, which proves chatbots are a boon to humankind.

Build a Superhuman Human Resource Team Using AI Chatbots

Human Resources, like Internal Communications, is considered to be underrated by other departments because the nature of the work being performed is administrative. The functioning of a department depends on the technology and methodologies used in day-to-day operations, which lead to a greater—in this case, employee—experience. It is time for support functions such as Human Resources to be robust, efficient, and smooth in its operations using modern technology, thereby reaching a state of digital transformation.

Different departments in organizations have adopted digital transformation to create better employee experiences, but Human Resources has lagged behind compared to other departments as a result of strict processes and company policies to deliver standardized results. In general, it is said that Human Resource professionals spend most of their time conducting transactional and administrative activities, and their remaining time on strategy and talent management. With so much variation in operations, how can Human Resources can be part of a strategic business transformation? Today, Human Resources is engaged in performing multiple routine tasks that can be automated using chatbots, which will free up employees to tackle more challenging work. Unless all departments are transformed digitally, we cannot conclude an organization is transformed.

The Ulrich Model of Human Resource Delivery

According to David Ulrich, who is known as the father of modern Human Resources, there is a new directive for Human Resources wherein the chief executive officer and the upper management team in Human Resources must become Human Resource champions. They must believe that the competitive success of the Human Resource function is essential to organizational excellence. And Human Resource employees must be accountable for delivering it.

Ulrich describes four important roles in which each member of the Human Resource team can deliver organizational excellence:

1. *Strategy execution:* Human Resources should operate in collaboration with senior and line managers in strategy execution, facilitating movement of planning from the conference room to the marketplace.

2. *Human Resource experts:* Without undermining the overall contribution of Human Resource professionals, it is high time that Human Resource employees get opportunities to become experts in the way of working and executing tasks in innovative ways to ensure that costs are reduced while quality is high.

3. *Employee-first mind-set:* Human Resources should become a champion for employees by presenting their concerns to senior management while working to enhance employee contributions to the organization.

4. *Continuous transformation:* Human Resource personnel should become agents of continuous transformation, shaping processes and creating a culture that helps to improve an organization's capacity for change.

In addition to these roles, as organizations mature, they must demand Human Resources to be a strategic partner and monitor closely the pulse of the employee workforce (i.e., company).

Forwardthinking executives and Human Resource leaders must recognize the different demands of a future workforce and workplace, and acknowledge that technology, applied in the right way, empowers employees and workplaces to be superagile and to achieve significantly more. This leadership will ultimately drive Human Resource transformation and finally turn the Ulrich model into a digital delivery model a model that pushes Human Resources to the next frontier using people analytics and conversational AI.

Different expectations of workforces and workplaces must be recognized by Human Resource executives, and the right technology and methodologies must be adopted to meet employee expectations. Workplaces must be agile, and the workforce must be collaborative to empower organizational transformation. Leadership is key in driving the Ulrich model and then turning this model into one that pushes Human Resources toward the next horizon. Use of technology such as chatbots will make Human Resources the next generation of strategic Human Resource partners of business units.

The following sections describe ways in which chatbots can used in Human Resource functions. The discussion shows how Human Resources can complete transactional Human Resource inquiries efficiently, and offer better opportunities to employees and managers.

Recruitment

Bulk hiring may create scaling issues. Chatbots can help in the resumé screening process and by getting information on prospective employees. Furthermore, the can perform background checks.

Onboarding

Chatbots used for onboarding make life easy because they are used to connect new employees with onshore and offshore teams, and allows them to interact with software such as Peoplesoft, Kronos, and Workday.

FAQs on Company Policies

Dedicated Human Resource teams spend huge amounts of time monitoring e-mail and responding to employee queries within a stipulated time frame. However, this manual way of working does not bring about a good end user experience because of delays resulting from the sheer volume of the number of requests and limited availability of Human Resource personnel. Chatbots, however, can answer FAQs posed by employees almost immediately 24/7.

Human Resource Chatbots for Subcontractors, Suppliers, and Partners

Chatbots can be deployed to communicate effectively between employees and subcontractors, suppliers, and partners.

Employee Training

Human Resource training using chatbots has become very effective because it involves more interactive participation from employees, not just sitting through a standard training video or watching a PowerPoint presentation.

Common Questions

In general, employees spend many hours each month searching for basic company-related information. Chatbots would quickly help employees find the answers they are looking for, making them more productive and satisfied.

Benefits Enrollment

Benefits enrollment is one of the most confusing, challenging, and frustrating tasks for Human Resource personnel. Employees spend large amounts of time understanding the process and submitting the required information.

Annual Self-assessments and Reviews

According to the Ulrich Model of Human Resources Delivery, more than 58% of Human Resource leaders say that the traditional review process is outdated and ineffective. Chatbots will allow for an instant exchange of feedback and performance insights with employees to help them be the best at what they do.

AI Chatbots Are Strategic Human Resource Partners

As the world begins to embrace the benefits of AI and intelligent enterprise automation, chatbots are emerging as an Agile solution for elevating employee experiences and optimizing transactional activities within Human Resources.

Per survey results published in the ServiceNow blog available at
chatbotsmagazine.com, 92% of Human Resource leaders want to provide
an elevated experience for their employees by using chatbots. In addition,
more than two-thirds of Human Resource leaders believe employees are
quite comfortable accessing chatbots to get desired information (Figure 8-
1). Human Resource leaders also predict that, by 2020, more than 75%
of employees will use chatbots for administrative or tractional Human
Resource queries. With the development of chatbots, Human Resource
teams can focus more on strategic activities rather than operational ones.

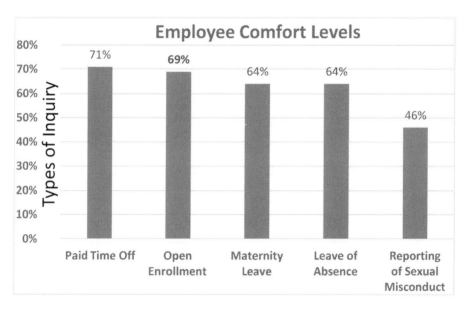

Figure 8-1. *Survey responses by Human Resource leaders*

With help from AI chatbots, Human Resource teams will finally be
able to move from an operational focus to a strategic one, and can impact
the organization at a greater level. The graphs in the following section,
from Kevin Kramer's report (chatbotsmagazine.com), show how Human
Resources today compare with Human Resources of the future using AI
chatbots.

The Future of Human Resources

As seen in Figure 8-2, there is a list of Human Resource activities: administration, transaction, talent and performance, and strategy. Activities linked to strategy are accomplished the least because of the other activities.

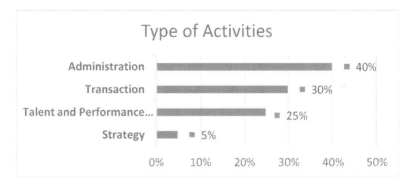

Figure 8-2. *Human Resources without chatbots*

In Figure 8-3, you can see that more time is spent on strategy after chatbots have been deployed.

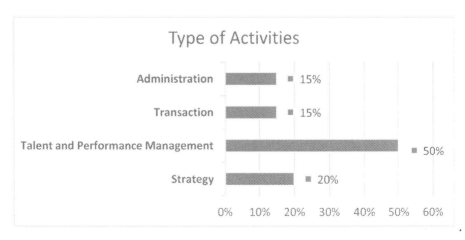

Figure 8-3. *Human Resources with chatbots*

Based on these figures, it is evident there will be a paradigm shift after the introduction of chatbots in Human Resources, and Human Resource high-value work, which could comprise 70% of Human Resource efforts. This does not mean that Human Resource teams can ignore administrative and tractional activities, which involves give and take, that are part of their work, but Human Resources can reply on chatbots to execute most of them, which will free up their time to perform strategic work. Consequently, Human Resources will become data driven, will focus on the employee experience, and will achieve operational excellence.

Data-driven Human Resources using chatbots will gain visibility in enterprise-wide conversations. With such an approach, we would expect Human Resource managers to effect the production of chatbots with a focus on data in order to change or improve company policies.

Human Resource teams adopting chatbots will achieve a personalized, instant employee experience. Employees can find answers to their questions using chatbots instead of using e-mail or making phone calls. They can communicate with a friendly chatbot using their preferred method, such as mobile, voice, or Web.

Human Resource teams will be digitally transformed and hence will achieve operational excellence. Chatbots can be deployed at a fraction of the cost and are available 24/7, 365 days a year. Money saved from implementing chatbots can be used for other Human Resource initiatives to focus on strategic goals and improve the employee experience.

The Millennial AI Chatbot Workforce

According to the Dell Future Workforce Study (`www.emc.com`), "the future workforce will be more mobile and supported by an array of digital technologies . . . with Millennials taking the global reins on the introduction and adoption of new technology."

According to a Brookings report (www.brookings.edu), millennials will comprise more than one in three adult Americans by 2020, and 75% of the workforce by 2025. Despite such major shifts in enterprises and trends, organizations are still waiting to embrace the digital-savvy workers of the future.

Traditional Workplace of Today

Today's workplace is still old-school (Figure 8-4). In fact, the average enterprise has nearly 700 apps and legacy software systems that are used for employee communication and collaboration with very few, if any, self-service options.

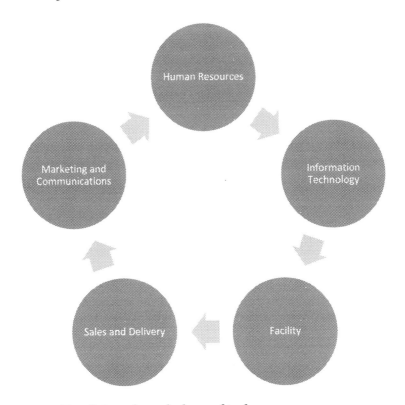

Figure 8-4. *Traditional workplace of today*

Organizations still prefer such systems or even unsupported vendor products, citing cost reasons. None of these systems is conducive to employee collaboration, nor do they have self-service options. With such constraints, employees are forced to follow workflows that are time-consuming and inefficient to gather the right information at the right time and from the right person.

According to a McKinsey report (`blog.xenit.eu`), "employees spend 1.8 hours every day—9.3 hours per week, on average—searching and gathering information. Put another way, businesses hire 5 employees but only 4 show up to work; the fifth is off searching for answers, but not contributing any value." Earlier, I mentioned that 75% of the workforce will be digital-savvy millennials by 2025. So, do we still anticipate productivity of employees to be driven by workflow or by introductive AI technology such as chatbots to access information in the most intelligent way? Per the Dell Future Workforce Study (`www.dell.com`), for enterprises to remain competitive, they must invest in smarter workplace technology to build a digital workforce that is more mobile, productive, and capable. By being mobile, face-to-face collaboration will decline, but collaboration will increase with the help of technology. Being productive implies the digital workforce will be digitally connected and will be better able to produce faster output. Being capable implies the digital workforce will use AI technology to achieve business goals.

Chatbots and conversational AI bring unique opportunities for enterprises to drive digital transformation across all departments, including Human Resources, IT, Facility, Sales and Delivery, Marketing and Communications, and Legal (Figure 8-5). By using AI technology such as chatbots, enterprises can create a more unified and flexible workplace in the future.

Figure 8-5. *Workplace of the future*

The workplace of the future will use chatbots as part of the organization to resolve business queries and achieve organizational goals. Say goodbye to the days when many workplace apps were required to accomplish different tasks. The workforce of the future will streamline communication across each area of the enterprise to execute daily tasks.

Summary

With this, we come to the end of this chapter and the end of this book. In this chapter, we looked at how we can achieve digital transformation by creating elevated customer and employee experiences.

I hope you enjoyed reading this book and have learned from it. For feedback or suggestions, please write to me at charles.waghmare@gmail.com.

Index

A

Adaptive cards, 90

Adhoc private messages, 110

Agile methodology, 52

AI applications
    cognitive services, 17
    expert system, 3
    gaming, 2
    IBM Watson, 4, 5
    intelligent robots, 4
    NLP, 2, 3
    vision system, 4

Alexa, 10, 154

Animation cards, 91

Artificial general intelligence, 9

Artificial Narrow
       Intelligence (ANI), 9

Artificial superhuman
       intelligence, 10

Audio cards, 92

Authorization code grant, 118

Azure chatbots, connecting with
    channels, 112, 113
    communication apps, 111, 112
    Cortana (*see* Cortana)
    direct line, 130–133
    Facebook Messenger, 135–141
    Facebook workplace, 141–143
    GroupMe, 143–145
    Office 365 e-mail, 134, 135
    Skype, 119–121
    Telegram Messenger app, 121,
       122, 124, 126
    webhooks, 138

Azure Search
    faceting values, 184
    search index, 183

B

Backup and disaster recovery, 18

BotFather, visit, 122

Bot navigation
    captain obvious, 84, 85
    clueless, 83
    mysterious, 84
    stubborn, 82
    unforgetting chatbot, 85, 86

Boxever, 7

Business
    benefits, 148, 149
    Casper, 37
    consumers, 38
    curiosity, 39
    customer expectations, 32

© Charles Waghmare 2019
C. Waghmare, *Introducing Azure Bot Service*,
https://doi.org/10.1007/978-1-4842-4888-1

D

E

Printed in the United States
By Bookmasters